IT SEEMED LIKE A GOOD IDEA . . .

A Cautionary Guide to 101 of Life's Potentially Most-Regrettable Decisions

D1289609

MEGHAN ROWLAND & CHRIS TURNER-NEAL

▲adamsmedia
AVON, MASSACHUSETTS

Published by
Adams Media, a division of F+W Media, Inc.
57 Littlefield Street, Avon, MA 02322. U.S.A.
www.adamsmedia.com

ISBN 10: 1-4405-3365-2
ISBN 13: 978-1-4405-3365-5
eISBN 10: 1-4405-3373-3
eISBN 13: 978-1-4405-3373-0

Printed in the United States of America.

10   9   8   7   6   5   4   3   2   1

Library of Congress Cataloging-in-Publication Data
Rowland, Meghan.
It seemed like a good idea—/Meghan Rowland and Chris Turner-Neal.
p. cm.
ISBN 978-1-4405-3365-5 (pbk.)—ISBN 1-4405-3365-2 (pbk.)—ISBN 978-1-4405-
3373-0 (ebook)—ISBN 1-4405-3373-3 (ebook)
1. Life skills—Handbooks, manuals, etc.—Humor. 2. Conduct of life—Humor.
I. Turner-Neal, Chris. II. Title.
PN6231.L49R69 2011
818'.602–dc23
2011049826

This book is available at quantity discounts for bulk purchases.
For information, please call 1-800-289-0963.

Dedicated to the memory of Rue McClanahan.
"Play it again, Blanche . . ."

ACKNOWLEDGMENTS

Our warmest thanks go to everyone at Adams Media, especially our editors Matt Glazer and Wendy Simard. Thank you to Richard and Diane Rowland, who let us live in their basement, eat their food, and harass their cat as we worked on this book. Thanks to Talia Warsaw, Sarah Gmeiner, and Rebecca Rowland for the inspiration. Finally, we are deeply grateful to the Insane Clown Posse and the good people at the Olney, Maryland, Giant grocery store for keeping us going.

Contents

Introduction

The Butterfly Effect: It's Complicated

"The best-laid schemes of mice and men are apt to go awry, and leave us naught but grief and pain for promised joy." —ROBERT BURNS

"Shit happens." —AMERICAN PROVERB

In a tulip field in Holland, a butterfly flutters its wings before coming to rest on a vivid red bloom. The tiny breeze produced by the butterfly's wings develops into a stronger gust, which joins with a gale crossing the North Sea. The gale reaches London, and on its merry way down Sloane Street playfully blows a young woman's skirt up, revealing her saucy knickers. A passing truck—sorry, *lorry*—driver becomes distracted by the view, and goes careening into one of the struts supporting the London Eye, the giant Ferris wheel by the Thames, knocking the wheel free. It rolls through the streets, causing a mild, very British panic, before coming to rest against Big Ben. Big Ben begins to lean, then topples, the spire shish-kabobing a family of Japanese tourists and a minor royal on the way down. As the dust clears, John Cleese is heard quietly remarking, "And now for something completely different." The insurance claims for the incident bankrupt the venerable firm Lloyd's of London, which pulls the entire British economy along in its death spiral. As Britain goes, so do all the major markets, and a week later people are grabbing their guns and driving Ford Falcons across the outback in search of oil.

It's called the butterfly effect—given a complex and sensitive enough system, small changes produce immense and unpredictable changes. The butterfly didn't *mean* to curb stomp London. Like all Dutch butterflies, it was tired and hungry from all the free socialized marijuana and prostitutes, and just wanted to chill out on a flower and snag a quick nectar fix before going back to its summer job at the Anne Frank House. But as the butterfly learned, even a common everyday activity like grabbing lunch before work can have outrageous, unforeseen consequences.

You are like this little butterfly, not only because you've blossomed into one of nature's most beautiful wonders, but because you have little to no control over the consequences of your actions. Think of it as a particularly terrifying aspect of karma. What this realization lacks in comfort it makes up for in amusement; if your life is basically a series of random events, so is everyone else's—but it's funnier when it happens to someone else! Read on for 101 tales of absurd results from everyday activities, all of which seemed like good ideas. . . .

They weren't.

CHAPTER 1

Three Raisinettes in Each Nostril and a Matt LeBlanc Tattoo

Bad Decisions and the Body

Most bad decisions, however serious they seem at the time, can be forgotten with a little work and a heart-to-heart with your old friend Jack Daniel. Blow your life savings investing in an all-natural herbal "male enhancement" supplement? Buy a Suze Orman book and get a second job at Kinko's—in time your credit score will iron itself out. Get a third strike shoplifting candy from Costco? Find religion during your time in prison and wait for a Democrat to get elected, then throw the metaphorical jailhouse doors wide open.

When the body is involved, however, it's a whole different story. The human body is a veritable museum of a lifetime of half-baked decision making. Each scar, stretch mark, and whimsical piercing tells a story—and nine times out of ten, that story is called "It Seemed Like a Good Idea" and includes the phrase, "but you learn from your mistakes."

Go to an All-You-Can-Eat Buffet

If there's anything on God's earth better than an all-you-can-eat buffet, you want it hunted down, shot, and served in a chafing dish next to the Mongolian beef. You're an American, dammit, and it's your God-given right to go to a place full of food you don't need and stuff it into your body like sausage into a casing. It's Tuesday and you're alive: time to go to Golden Corral.

One Hour Later

As you stir a handful of fried popcorn shrimp into a bowl of mashed potatoes, some fat guy sticks a microphone in your face and bellows, "Ma'am! Ma'am, what are you eating? Ma'am, do you know that two-thirds of the population of Myanmar lives on less than four hundred calories a day? Ma'am!" You consider sticking a pork chop in his mouth to shut him up, but then you wouldn't have the pork chop. You suddenly recognize gadfly and documentarian Michael Moore, who—according to his T-shirt—is preparing a new project called *The Lard-Spangled Banner* about Americans' eating habits. You grab the mic from him as though it were a drumstick and deliver a heartfelt speech about how your grandfather didn't storm Okinawa so you could sit around eating cabbage water and imitation pork, and that if Moore doesn't like it here, he can check out the menu options in Red China.

Seven Months Later

Your speech makes it into the final cut of *The Lard-Spangled Banner*, and your deep-fried libertarian tirade strikes a chord with conservatives. As "Kendra the Eater," you replace "Joe the Plumber" as a Tea Party darling.

Nine Months Later

The Tea Party books you a spot at the American Food and Diet Convention, hoping your presence there will unsettle the "Communist" pro-vegetable lobby. After a heated panel discussion on whether it's even theoretically possible to make kale appetizing, you lock eyes with a tall, distinguished-looking man. With a start, you recognize him as Jared Fogle, of Subway Diet fame. Bashfully, he approaches you and invites you out for a drink.

Two Years Later

A romance has blossomed, and you marry Jared so the country can heal. The reception is held at an area Subway, where you order a Meatball Supreme, and Jared orders his usual Veggie Delite. This display of unconditional love calms the frenzied American political climate, allowing for the election of a broad unity government that leads our great nation to an ever-more-glorious future.

Reproduce

Looking for a tax deduction, an excuse to watch more *Sesame Street*, and something to occupy your wife's time so she doesn't nag you while you're trying to do jigsaw puzzles? It's time to get your breed on.

One Year Later

You've had a fair amount of fun trying, but you haven't been able to conceive, so you make an appointment with a fertility specialist.

One Year, One Week Later

You go to the fertility doctor, and all goes well at first. He asks you a number of questions, then mentions that he's going to need a "sample." He calls for a nurse, who escorts you down the hall to a small private room. "This is where the magic happens," she announces, "need any supplies?" You say "yes," more to see what she means than anything else, and she excuses herself briefly and returns with a stack of skin rags and a little sample cup. The nurse tells you to "knock 'em dead, tiger," then shuts the door behind her.

One Year, One Week, Fifteen Minutes Later

Free porn is free porn, but if you're in a situation where you need men to get off in a hurry, maybe you should have something a little racier than early '90s editions of *Oui* and *High Society*. All the women have Aqua-Netted bangs, brightly colored scrunchies, and nervous smiles. The general effect is very "Kelly Kapowski Made Some Mistakes" and it's not getting you where you need to be.

One Year, One Week, Thirty Minutes Later

Just when you are really getting on the road, the nurse taps on the door and asks if you are all right. If "all right" means "trying to masturbate into a cup in a doctor's office to the thought of my wife and Topanga from *Boy Meets World* drinking a few vodka tonics and giving in to curiosity," then sure, otherwise, *stop tapping on the door.*

One Year, One Week, Forty-Five Minutes Later

You're getting desperate. Farrah Fawcett in the red swimsuit? No, too dead. Bo Derek running along the beach in *10*? No, too dated. Sharon Stone flashing her beav in *Basic Instinct?* Too crazy! Dammit! As the nurse taps on the door *again*, you panic, grab the Go-Gurt you keep in your backpack for blood sugar emergencies, squirt a healthy dollop into the sample cup, and toss it at the nurse as you run out.

One Year, One Week, Four Hours Later

You dread explaining everything to your wife, so you take your time getting home. When you arrive, your wife informs you that the fertility clinic called and told her that you had either given them a sample of yogurt or were "some kind of magical dairy creature." She now no longer thinks you're mature enough to have a child, and has bought you a hermit crab to practice nurturing until you can act like an adult.

Develop Your Mind

Oh, butterfingers. You accidentally clicked on a pop-up ad. You move to close the window out, but then pause. You *don't* know your IQ. You *do* wonder about how it affects your life and relationships. You *would* be willing to watch a short advertisement for Dove products in order to be granted access to a short, accurate online intelligence test. After learning about Dove's new PMS relief body wash, you take the test (which is surprisingly difficult) and learn that your IQ is 86, a mere sixteen points above being legally dead. Apparently you're not only no Einstein, you're not even a Jeff Foxworthy. You decide to try to claw your way up to at least Lassie level by reading the great works of world literature. You download literary critic Harold Bloom's list of the Western canon of world literature, and start at the top.

One Week Later
Oedipus Rex: You write an anonymous letter to your mother asking her to please tone down the eye makeup at family functions. She recognizes your handwriting and an awkward e-mail exchange ensues.

Two Weeks Later
Medea: You apologize to your mother.

Three Weeks Later
Titus Andronicus: You embrace veganism, just in case.

Four Weeks Later
Native Son: You resolve that, in case you should happen to commit a murder in the future, you will just throw the body in the river. No muss, no fuss.

Five Weeks Later

Angels in America: You buy an economy pack of condoms and promise yourself you'll wear one. Every time.

Six Weeks Later

Great Expectations: You delete your ex's number from your phone. Sometimes it just doesn't work out, and you need to be strong and move on.

Seven Weeks Later

Huckleberry Finn: You realize, finally, that it's okay to say it if you have a black friend.

Eight Weeks Later

Garfield Shovels It In (His 51st Book): You needed a break.

Nine Weeks Later

Lolita: You make a note to yourself to start checking IDs when you pick up girls at the bar.

Ten Weeks Later

The Grapes of Wrath: You reconsider your stance on late-term abortions.

Eleven Weeks Later

Catcher in the Rye: You look for your gun, and wonder where does that son of a bitch Ringo Starr hang out?

Two Years Later

Having finished reading all of the heavyweights of Western literature, you retake the IQ test. Since you missed the point of every single work, your score remains unchanged, and you've wasted the past two years of your life reading instead of going cougar hunting at Applebee's. Then again, at least you recognize the Gore Vidal quote on the website.

Shave Your Legs

Everyone's talking about body acceptance these days. With the world economy still locked in its room blasting Morrissey and refusing to come out, no one can afford cosmetic surgery or elaborate beauty treatments, and many people have let their gym memberships lapse in favor of jerry-rigging some ankle weights with duct tape and two cans of off-brand creamed corn. Now that we all look like mug shots, we try to comfort each other with unrealistic verbal butterfly kisses like "natural beauty" and "inner poise," and loudly proclaim that fat can be sexy and that you only get really *good* dye jobs when you do it yourself with a quart of hydrogen peroxide from the gas station. The crown jewel in these natural beauty arguments is always "Women are supposed to have body hair." It's always some cute little blond Wellesley girl with two oh-so-adorable tiny patchlets of oh-so-adorable blond hair you see in her underarms as she raises her protest sign. This may work for the co-eds, but your grandmother was from Russia, where the women have evolved heavy pelts to confuse invading tribes. You might not be able to afford laser hair removal treatments anymore, and waxing might now be a special treat, but you're going to empty your change jar, buy a Lady Bic razor, and shave your legs.

One Minute Later
Of course, you nick yourself immediately.

Four Minutes Later
Still bleeding.

Ten Minutes Later
Still bleeding. You have had *periods* shorter than this.

Forty-Five Minutes Later

It's not a heavy flow of blood, but it is *remarkably* persistent. You've bled through a box of generic Band-Aids. Annoyed, you go to the emergency room to forestall the small but increasing chance of starring in a new urban legend, The Lady Who Bled to Death Shaving Her Legs.

Three Hours Later

The doctor has managed to stop the bleeding by wrapping your knee with the entire annual cotton yield of a midsized Southern state. He wants to take some blood—"don't worry, there's enough lying around I can use"—and send it to the lab to see why you're gushing like a fine new oil well.

One Week Later

After a week spent walking around v-e-r-y c-a-r-e-f-u-l-l-y, you go back to the doctor for a follow-up. He sits you down and explains that adult-onset hemophilia is incredibly rare in women, and has in fact only been reported in one family: those celebrated bleeders and Tsars of all the Russias, the Romanovs. Suddenly Grandma Anastasia's insistence that the Mary Kay lady curtsy to her before bringing out the samples seems marginally less insane. You have the doctor send a sample of your DNA to Moscow for confirmation, and on the way home max out your credit card on a fur hat and a CD of Tchaikovsky's symphonies.

Five Years Later

The blood test came back, and it turns out you *are* the last Romanov princess. You have spent five years mortgaging everything you own to hire lawyers to sue the Russian government to give you back your family's "damn fancy eggs!" Lenin is giggling in his grave.

Meditate

Your doctor has some bad news. It appears that a lifetime of "bacon ranch" products, referring to carrying beer from the truck into the house as "a workout," and rooting for the perennially disappointing Tampa Bay Buccaneers has pushed your blood pressure to the breaking point. Your doctor advised you to lose some weight, and even showed you a model of what five pounds of fat looks like; you offered to bring in a deep fryer and show him how to use the fat to make corn dogs. Dr. Huang did not seem to think this was as funny as you did, but said that if you were unwilling to lose weight you might be able to lower your blood pressure through meditation. You're willing to try anything other than changing your diet, exercising, or calming down, and you do like any activity that can be performed while sitting motionless.

One Week Later

Your copy of *Meditation for Dummies* arrives in the mail. You flip through it while idly watching *Die Hard* and eating some frozen jalapeño poppers. It seems pretty simple. All you have to do is sit there, clear your mind of extraneous thoughts, and attune yourself to the cosmos? Isn't that just what masturbation is?

Two Weeks Later

You seem to really have a knack for meditation. It's already helping your blood pressure, and would probably help it even more if you didn't insist on doing your deep breathing through a Marlboro Red.

Three Weeks Later

While you're meditating in front of the TV, your son comes in and asks if you're watching NASCAR. You ask him if we can truly know whether we are watching NASCAR or whether NASCAR is watching us. He says fine, he'll just ask Mom for a ride to the mall.

Four Weeks Later

Your wife asks you what you want for dinner, and you reply that "wanting" is the root of all unhappiness and pain in the universe. She smacks you on the back of the head and makes only enough Chicken Parmesan for herself and the kids.

Five Weeks Later

You're really on a roll. You're in a deeper state of meditation than ever before, layers and layers of consciousness peeling back from reality. You realize that you're approaching Nirvana, the state of perfect peace, tranquility, connectedness, and nothingness striven for by devotees of Eastern religion. As your breathing stops and your physical body dies, and your soul melts into the oneness of creation, your last conscious thought is that you forgot to pick up your dry cleaning.

Get a Piercing

After failing out of Barbizon Modeling School, you were adrift. You've wanted to be a model since you were a little girl, but after flunking Advanced Poise and Remedial Staring into the Middle Distance, you feared your dream would be forever out of reach. One day, though, you had an epiphany. While doing a little online shopping, you came across a website that specialized in impractical, brightly colored leather accessories. You noticed that all the models on the site were tattooed, pierced, dyed, and generally eccentric looking—but hell, they had work! You decide to give "alternative modeling" a try, and think the best way to start would be by getting a piercing.

One Day Later

You arrive at Misty's Discount Pierce-a-torium, and decide to go large with a nose piercing. Misty, a peroxide blonde with sun-damaged skin and a sweet smile, grabs tongs and needle, and before you know it you are a bona fide pierced gal. You feel a little unsteady on your feet, but you chalk it up to the fact that you just had a metal ring forced through your nasal cartilage and toddle on home.

One Week Later

It's been a strange week. You've been seeing flashes of color; experiencing strange tastes, even when not eating; and even hearing things. You make an emergency appointment with your doctor, who can't find anything wrong with you. Concerned, he checks you into the hospital for further tests.

Two Weeks Later

The doctors have finally diagnosed you with synesthesia, a relatively uncommon neurological abnormality in which the sensory pathways are crossed, allowing people with synesthesia to "taste colors" or "see sounds." You have what is informally called "the whole shebang," a particularly complex case in which all stimuli you receive trigger secondary sensations. They have never seen it develop spontaneously in an adult, but do not believe you are in danger and send you home. You will never realize it, but your synesthesia was triggered when Misty pierced your septum and unwittingly struck a major acupuncture meridian, the "Highway of the Sensory Luck Dragon."

Three Weeks Later

You're at home, trying to figure out how to deal with your new synesthesia. It's not unpleasant, exactly, but it is very unnerving. You turn on the TV to distract yourself and catch a rerun of the crime drama *Law and Order: Special Victims Unit*. Amazingly, the sound of heartthrob Chris Meloni's voice triggers in your rewired mind the exact sensation of a satisfying pot roast dinner with all the trimmings. Since there's always an episode of *SVU* on, you flip from channel to channel, stuffing your metaphorical face with the meaty yet tender strains of Meloni's voice. You're so busy "eating" that you forget to eat and eventually starve to death.

Have a One-Night Stand

It's been nearly nine months since you've gotten laid. You've tried everything—granted, for you "everything" is JDate and volunteering one Saturday at the animal shelter, but a dry spell is a dry spell nonetheless. You've tried to work off the pent-up sexual energy with other activities, but there are only so many nights you can spend playing Grand Theft Auto and lifting weights. It doesn't look like a relationship is on the horizon any time soon, so you decide that what the doctor ordered is a good old-fashioned one-night stand.

One Day Later

You wax your knuckle hair, douse yourself with an alluring blast of Axe body spray, and hit a popular singles bar. You make some small talk with a woman, but she rejects your advances because your knuckles are too smooth and it looks effeminate.

One Week Later

After striking out more times than the Yeshiva University softball team, you decide to consult an expert, and buy a book by a man who claims to be a pickup expert who can seduce any woman.

Two Weeks Later

Per the pickup artist's advice, the next time you're at the bar you insult a girl to display dominance and get her attention. "Jugsy McArmfat" doesn't find your approach cute, and instead of following you home throws her Sea Breeze in your face.

Three Weeks Later

The insults didn't work, so you try the next strategy in the book. "Peacocking" is deliberately dressing in a garish and flashy manner to attract women's attention and start conversations. You go out in an "I'm with Stupid" T-shirt, a jester's hat, and heavy eyeliner. The only woman willing to talk to you hands you the card for a methadone clinic and tells you, "Where there's life, there's hope."

Four Weeks Later

You assume last week's failure stemmed from not peacocking "hard" enough, so you don a red wig and a French maid's outfit. As you approach the bar, a hot broad in sequined hot pants and a black tube top walks up to you and says "Hey, awesome, but we're meeting down the block. C'mon." You're not sure, but you think you just got recruited for an orgy.

Five Weeks Later

It turned out the woman in the hot pants was a *Rocky Horror Picture Show* fanatic on her way to a screening, and assumed you were, too. The first hour or so was pretty awkward, but now you're thoroughly engaged with the Rocky Horror lifestyle, and it fulfills you in ways a woman never could.

Get a Massage

You really took some tough hits during last week's club rugby game. It's been a few days, and your shoulder is still tight and sore. You've tried hot compresses, cold packs, stretches, Tylenol, and even visualizing the knotted muscles gently coming free like seeds blown off a dandelion, but nothing has helped. You decide to go ahead and book yourself a sports massage at a physical therapist's office.

Two Days Later

On the day of your appointment, you arrive a little early and leaf through the old magazines in the lobby. You're just beginning to work a corner of the *People* crossword puzzle when the therapist comes for you. She is, in plain English, the most attractive woman you've ever seen, sort of a Helen of Troy with cleavage. You think the massage might be pretty enjoyable after all.

Five Minutes Later

You've stripped down to a towel and lain on the massage table. Facedown, fortunately: you've developed an erection from the attractive therapist's proximity and would rather not have that conversation just now.

Ten Minutes Later

You realize it's been six months since Barbara, and no one after that. The massage is doing wonders for your shoulder, but it's also having some dramatic effects farther south.

Twenty Minutes Later

You tried to stop yourself, but couldn't keep from ejaculating into your towel. You try, with reasonable success, to at least do so silently. Your shoulder is getting loose, but everything else is tensed up. How on earth are you going to get this evidence (towel) out of here?

Thirty Minutes Later

Your massage is over, and the therapist tells you to lie on the table and relax for a few minutes if you need to. As soon as she leaves you alone, you hurriedly dress and mull your options. You decide the best defense is a good offense, and plan to nonchalantly carry the towel out with you as though you'd had it all along.

Forty Minutes Later

After you pay, the receptionist smiles and reaches for your towel. You panic and say the first thing that comes to mind, which unfortunately is: "Oh, no, this is mine. It's not a towel, it's . . . a turban. I'm a Sikh. Better pop this baby back on." You hurriedly knot it around your head and bolt for the door.

Three Days Later

You send a check for $5 to the physical therapist to replace the towel, and a check for $500 to the local Sikh community center to apologize for appropriating their cultural heritage to get you out of a sticky situation. They are mystified, but can afford to have the pool table re-felted now.

Get a Hot Tub

You recently came into a tidy sum of money when your uncle died and left you his fortune. Per the will: "To my nephew Eric, I leave my entire estate. I don't really like you much, Eric, but I dislike your mother much more. Spend this on something that'll piss her off. Love, Uncle Steve." That's all the encouragement you needed. As soon as the will was probated and you had access to the funds, you went out and bought the gaudiest, most ostentatious, most lavish luxury item your fevered little brain could think of: a black, eight-person hot tub with built-in margarita maker. Granted, this is a very "cocaine mogul in South Florida in 1987" idea of luxury, but you draw a disproportionate number of your life lessons from *Scarface*.

One Day Later

Your mother is furious that you wasted so much on a hot tub when there are starving children in India and she hasn't had a new dress in months. You tell her, "Settle down, toots," and pass her a C-note. She beelines it to the closest Dress Barn.

One Week Later

You start tanning pretty heavily at the salon. If you're going to be out in your hot tub all the time, you don't want to scare all the babes away with your pasty torso.

Two Weeks Later

You go ahead and invest in a Speedo—black, though, so it's not tacky. You refer to it as your "banana hammock" in front of your mother, who is appalled until you give her a little more Dress Barn money.

Three Weeks Later

You decide to grow the chest hair you normally shave to accent your new accessory, a large gold medallion. You go ahead and let your shoulder hair grow in, too. Natural is beautiful.

Four Weeks Later

Wait, what? There's an old-fashioned singles bar called "Mingle's" out by the airport? You start going there nightly to meet chicks to invite back to your pad for cocktail parties. You alternate between two pickup lines: "What's your sign?" and "I have a hot tub." You bat about .600 with these.

Five Weeks Later

You neighbors call in a noise complaint against you because you're having a bikini hot tub party with a handful of sleazy broads and have been playing "Mack the Knife" on loop for three hours. You tell them to lighten up and live a little.

Six Weeks Later

Your mother comes to confront you about the fact that you've become one of those tacky, hairy, overtanned men who wear gaudy jewelry and spend every waking moment trying to coax trashy dames into their hot tubs. You see why your uncle couldn't stand her. You think about her words for a while, then realize you're rich and don't have to give a shit what she thinks. You may keep getting the same case of gonorrhea from the same sleazy broads, and your fortune may be rapidly dwindling due to high maintenance costs, but you've found your destiny—as Hot Tub Guy. Pass the margaritas, Starla.

Experiment with Homosexuality

You don't know if it's the warm spring air, the changing social attitudes, or the fact that Ryan Gosling appears in practically every movie these days, but you've been questioning your sexuality recently. Are tits really that great, or do you just think they are because they endorse so many of your favorite beers? You've become increasingly unsettled, and you realize that the only way to know for sure is to experiment a little and see how you feel. You find a nice guy on a dating site and ask him out.

Two Hours Later

Ashton is a perfect gentleman. He pulls out your chair, makes recommendations on the menu without being pushy, and at the end of the evening gives you a sweet but intense goodnight kiss.

Three Weeks Later

Ashton's lovemaking is tender without being dull and passionate without being controlling. You wake up the next day in his arms, and notice that while you slept, he snuck out to buy you flowers.

Six Months Later

You tell your parents you've fallen in love with a man. Your mother embraces you and tells you she prayed you'd find love. Your father shakes your hand and tells you the substance, not the form, is what matters, and he hopes your partnership is as good as his marriage. They can't wait to meet Ashton.

Three Years Later

After a late-night debate and last-minute vote in Richmond, marriage equality comes to Virginia, which now really is for lovers. You and Ashton marry on the veranda of a restored plantation house.

Seven Years Later

You decide to go for it. You and Ashton take out a small business loan and open a small knickknack and gift shop. It struggles for the first couple of years, but soon becomes a fixture in the revitalized downtown shopping district.

Fourteen Years Later

Using some of the profits from your store, you endow a shelter for runaway gay teens so that they will have a safe place to go.

Fifty-Seven Years Later

You pass away peacefully in your sleep. Ashton has been gone for about a year now, and as you die a smile lights your features, as you will soon be with him again.

An Eternity Later

You are burning in Hell. However, since all the other gay people are there too, it's not that bad. You all watch a lot of *Mommie Dearest* and have the occasional themed luau.

Get Acrylic Nails

When you were a little girl, you were always fascinated by women with long, manicured nails. Your mother worked in ceramics and always kept her nails short, but you'd see the bright talons on women in stores or restaurants and imagine what it would be like to have fancy nails of your own. You could gesture with them, you could tap things with them for emphasis, and you'd never again have trouble getting the first chunk of peel off an orange. You forgot about this by high school, but you recently went to a new hairstylist, and the sensation of her running her smooth acrylic nails along your scalp reminded you of your childhood wonderment. On a whim, you ask her to do your nails just like hers.

Two Hours Later

You've tapped every item in the house, both with the tip and the curved top of your nails. You spent a good fifteen minutes in front of the mirror, pointing at yourself and reciting lines from old Joan Crawford movies. You've peeled enough lemons to garnish a month's worth of Tom Collinses. You might have had all the fun you can with these nails unless you wind up with some poison ivy to scratch.

Four Hours Later

You try to call your credit card company to dispute a charge, but your nails slip on the phone keys and you inadvertently dial the Prison Pals Hotline, where lonely ladies meet fixer-uppers, and have a surprisingly interesting and open conversation with Adam, who's made some mistakes but is taking advantage of the prison's GED classes and Bible study.

Six Months Later

You and Adam have developed a valued phone friendship. "No, I agree with you. People can change. Prison should be about reform, not punishment. I'll talk to you next week."

Nine Months Later

Adam calls you from a pay phone and tells you he was unexpectedly paroled, and needs a place to crash. You hesitate, but decide the Christian thing to do would be to give him refuge in his distress. You give him your address and start making up the hide-a-bed.

Nine Months, Thirty Minutes Later

As soon as he arrives, you recognize him. "Adam" is actually Charlie Boone, the serial killer more commonly known as the Las Vegas Mangler. Quick as a flash he overpowers you and ties you to a dining room chair. He apologizes, but reiterates what he said at his trial: he likes killing more than being polite. He gags you and leaves to fetch his "apparatus."

Nine Months, Thirty-Two Minutes Later

Thank God you kept up with your nails! They add just enough length to your fingers that you're able to undo the knots and free yourself. You run for your gun and have a hard time guiding your nail through the trigger guard, but you're ready when Charlie comes back.

One Year Later

The mayor gives you a medal for shooting Charlie and saving the county the expense of a manhunt.

Babysit Your Nephew

Your sister has always been hesitant to ask you to babysit her three-year-old son, what with your chronic self-centeredness and history of falling asleep with your flat iron on, but desperate times call for desperate measures. She and her husband have tickets to see Margaret Cho, and with the rest of their usual sitters busy, it's come down to you or a random person from craigslist. When Hotmail temporarily went down earlier in the evening for routine maintenance, the gig officially became yours.

One Hour Later

You're forced to endure a mind-numbing twenty-minute lecture on how to properly administer an EpiPen but only half listen because you've seen *Pulp Fiction* like a hundred times.

One Hour and Thirty Minutes Later

You decide to make the most of the few remaining hours of daylight and take your nephew to the playground down the street. Truth be told, you've been craving the shit out of a good old-fashioned swing for months, but there's just something about a twenty-seven-year-old woman showing up to a playground by herself that's always seemed a little too creepy for your liking. You thank God your sister's IUD fell asleep at the wheel four years ago and gleefully hop on a swing next to your nephew.

One Hour and Forty-Five Minutes Later

The metal O-rings flanking either side of the swing's seat are digging into your ass and the entire apparatus is ominously creaking like the Titanic slowly sinking to its watery grave. You don't remember that happening when you were a kid. . . .

Two Hours Later

After managing to pry all of your person out of the swing set, you try going down the spiral slide with your nephew and end up getting stuck halfway down when the sudden twists and turns can't accommodate the "luxurious" girth of your thighs. Although the playground is clearly built for children, you've never felt so fat in your entire life. You decide it's time to lose some serious weight.

One Day Later

First stop of the day: GNC. If it killed Anna Nicole Smith or is being backed by a Kardashian—you'll take it in bulk.

One Week Later

You restrict your diet to two Altoids and a slice of Havarti cheese a day and begin grapevining everywhere to burn extra calories. Everyone agrees that you look insane but have *seriously* impressive rhythm.

One Month Later

You become totally "preoccupied with your weight" (which is Sorority House for "anorexic") and, desperate to lose even more weight, swallow a rubber Livestrong bracelet in a misguided attempt to perform a DIY lap band surgery. It backfires when you have to have it surgically removed and the hospital's IV gives you a ton of water weight.

Use a Neti Pot

Springtime in The Pollen Belt is a *bitch*. You haven't smelled anything since St. Patrick's Day and you leave a Gretel-like trail of used tissues in your wake everywhere you go. You lose so much mucus on a daily basis you'd think you'd be able to fit into your "Semester After I Had Mono Jeans," but they still just barely zip up. If Claritin were Quaaludes, you'd be an evening with Andy Warhol away from being the human embodiment of 1974. At this point you're so desperate, you'd even wash out your sinuses with salt water. As it turns out, there's a device that does just that and it's called the "neti pot." It looks like a teapot a genie would live in, but instead of rubbing it for three wishes, you use it to pour salt water in one nostril and out the other. People claim that the Hopi Indians invented the neti pot, and the Hopi Indians say, "You people are crazy. Get off my land." Either way, here you are in your bathroom with a spigot shoved in one nostril and a stream of water pouring out the other. You don't care what Cover Girl says—you are not beautiful right now.

Twenty Seconds Later

As the water winds its way through your mucus-filled sinuses, you suddenly remember a really funny *Roseanne* blooper and get the giggles.

Twenty-Two Seconds Later

"Oh God—something's going down the wrong pipe . . ."

Forty-Five Seconds Later

As you choke on several ounces of salt water and mucus, your vision begins to dim and you realize what's happening. With your last thought, you curse John Goodman, Katrina commercials be damned.

Forty-Six Seconds Later

Clad in white and glowing ethereally, you glare down at your corpse, which is wearing Scooby-Doo boxers and a torn sports bra.

Ten Minutes Later

At this point you don't know if you're going to heaven, hell, or the ill-defined Jewish afterlife, but you'd like your corpse to look a little more Sleeping Princess and a little less Mia Hamm on a bender.

One Day Later

Dropping by to borrow your curling iron and $45, your sister walks into the bathroom to find your ghost in an awkward position: shaving your corpse's bikini line. Through the doorway, however, it just looks like a depressing lesbian adventure and she backs out hurriedly saying, "SORRY. SORRY. I STILL LOVE YOU. SORRY."

Three Days Later

After your body is found in earnest, your sister's testimony leads your family and local police to believe you were murdered by your lesbian lover. An intense *wommon*-hunt ensues.

One Month Later

Doomed for eternity to haunt the bathroom where you died, you read a newspaper the new tenant has left on the floor and learn that you've been posthumously given the Ellen DeGeneres LGBTQ Hero Award.

Quit Smoking

When you took your first drag of a cigarette behind the gym at your eighth grade dance, you didn't do it because you wanted to be A Smoker. Being cool was an uphill battle for a flat thirteen-year-old girl with a mother who wouldn't let her bleach her moustache, despite the gym teacher's constant comments that "that one's coming in real nice, son. *Real* nice." If smoking made you look cooler and even a fraction less like John Oates, you were into it. Twenty years, a pair of respectable C-cups, and a biweekly standing appointment at House of Waxing later, and you still smoke like a chimney. Tired of not being able to open an e-mail from a loved one without seeing graphic photos of rotting lungs and gaping neck holes, you've decided to quit smoking. Congratulations! Today is the first day of the rest of your life.

Eight Hours Later

You would tongue-kiss a homeless man if it meant you could suck the nicotine out from between his teeth.

Three Days Later

You've tried the gum, the patch, electronic cigarettes, lollipops—everything. Nothing seems to work. Your nerves are frayed, and small, everyday annoyances get magnified in your head until they're on par with genocide.

Four Days Later

You snap in a business meeting and go on a tirade about how much you hate athletes who thank God for their sports victories: "Because people are starving in Darfur and sometimes children get cancer, but yes, God thought his best work could be done today at *Wimbledon*. You arrogant fuck."

"You arrogant fuck" still reverberating off the boardroom walls, you prepare yourself for the firing of a lifetime, but are instead met with boisterous laughter.

One Month Later

After nicotine-withdrawal-induced rants on the Oscars, fad diets, and Justine the emo graphics intern, your "raw" comedy style becomes legendary around the office and at your boss's behest you do an open mic at The Cincinnati Ha Ha.

One Year Later

Rolling Stone features you as one of their "Top 10 Up-and-Coming Comedians," dubbing you "Lewis Black in a Water Bra."

Ten Years Later

You've become one of the greatest comedians of your generation and have delighted audiences around the world with your angry, loud, and—more times than not—violent rants. Unfortunately, as a result of spending a decade being constantly livid, you develop severe hypertension, have a heart attack on stage after a particularly aggressive bit about unnecessarily complicated DVD menus, and die.

Ten Years and One Day Later

As you sit in heaven watching the U.S. Open with God, Allah, and Buddy Holly, you can't help but think that if you were just going to end up dying young from a heart attack anyway, you wish you could have done so with a cool, refreshing Virginia Slim in your mouth.

Run a Marathon

In 490 B.C., Athenian soldier Pheidippides was tasked with running the 26.2 miles from Marathon, Greece, to Athens to deliver word of the Greek victory. Pheidippides successfully ran the 26.2 miles, raised two devil-horned hands over his head, and promptly keeled over and died. Naturally, you will be attempting to run the same distance with your girlfriend because running a marathon together is a "bonding experience." Frankly, if you have to have an Ancient Greece–themed bonding experience, you'd rather try anal sex or go to war with Persia, but you're not calling the shots here. You arrive at the starting line ready to make Pheidippides jealous.

One Minute Later

You feel good. You feel ready. You're limbered up, you're full of carbs . . . and your nipple guards are at home on top of the fish tank. Shit. This is not going to feel pleasant, but surely the dangers of having a shirt rub across your nipples are overstated?

Twenty Minutes Later

Denver marathon master of ceremonies Brian Dennehy fires the starting pistol and you and your nipples are off.

Fifty Minutes Later

Mile 5: It's not that bad. It's borderline *sensual*, even erotic.

Two Hours, Ten Minutes Later

Mile 13: There's mild chafing, but no worse than a thorough hazing from the boys in Skull and Bones.

Two Hours, Forty Minutes Later

Mile 16: You know what it's like to have two furious sea crabs dangling from your nipples. Lucky you.

Four Hours and Twenty Minutes Later

You're about to cross the finish line and it's about goddamn time because you've got two bloody streaks going down your chest like a lactating vampire and with each step the invisible baby wolves you're apparently breastfeeding dig in a little deeper. As it turns out, you're not seeing double; the figure crossing the finish line ahead of you is in fact a set of Siamese twins who overcame the odds and finished a marathon. As they cross the finish line, a sea of photographers snap their photograph, which will run in papers worldwide tomorrow under headlines like "Two Heads, Two Legs, and Two Hearts Full of Determination." You will be in the background of all of these photographs with your flailing gait and weeping nipples.

One Week Later

Inspired by your bloody fashion "choice," Lady Gaga adopts your look and makes twin streaks of beef blood down the front of your blouse the new hot accessory for fall. She asks you, a gay witch, and Dr. Teeth and the Mayhem to form her entourage at this year's MTV Video Music Awards. You accept.

Get a Tan

Irish heritage has its pros and cons. On the plus side, you are descended from an ancient race of noble warriors and mystical bards, and have both a cultural imperative to drink heavily and an almost preternatural ability to fulfill it. Less rewarding are the all-tuber all-the-time cuisine, Catholic doctrine, and skin so fair doctors only charge you half price for an X-ray. Forget nuclear weapons and bioengineered plagues—the real terrorist threat to Ireland is someone with a portable sun lamp. You thought you'd resigned yourself to wearing a T-shirt into the pool and a tracksuit to the beach, but yesterday, as you opened up your parasol to walk across the street to buy cigarettes, something snapped. You only have one life, and you're going to spend at least a few days of it with a killer tan.

One Day Later

You choose to start small, and at the tanning salon ask for the shortest period possible on the lowest power possible. Lo and behold, by the time you arrive home from "UV Ray's Discount Tans" your entire body has become a uniform, perfect pink. Add a nonthreatening demeanor and wacky hair and you'd be set for a Halloween costume as a background character from *Doug*, but as it is you'll have to spend the next three days nude except for a damp sheet.

One Week Later

After you peel off all your dead skin, molting like a crab, you slather your new skin in an "X-treem" sunless tanning lotion you found online while healing. Except for the phrase "As brown like your friend wouldn't be believing," all the writing on the bottle is in a language you expertly identify as Finnish, or something (anything with that many dots can't be wrong). Eighteen coats later, you are a bronze goddess.

Two Weeks Later

A dozen roses from Vittorio, the gorgeous Italian you met at the club last night! You feel a little dishonest: He came up to you and introduced himself because, in his words, he "had to meet a girl with such beautiful Italian coloring," and you panicked and introduced yourself as "Bridget Sullivanizzi." Well, you'll tell him eventually. You have lots more self-tanner, and roses!

Two Years Later

You really should have told Vittorio you weren't Italian before you married him. Not only do you feel guilty, you're running out of the case of tanner you bought, and you can't get more because according to the website, "this page no longer exists." Maybe you can just . . . gracefully fade and let the truth out slowly.

Two Years, Six Months Later

Vittorio, sobbing, bursts into your room juggling a mallet, stake, and crucifix, shouting, "I love you, I'm sorry, but I have to." Your skin faded so fast and so far that—along with your inability to digest garlic, what with being a "potato person" and all—it convinced him that you were a vampire. Not anemic, not sick, a fucking *vampire*. You narrowly avoid being staked, but it quickly becomes clear that you are a liar, he is an idiot, and this marriage is doomed. You think, not for the first time, that you should have just tried going blonde.

Get a Nose Job

It's not that you were unattractive growing up, exactly. Ninety-five percent of you was actually pretty cute, but you had quite the beak on you. You tried to take it in stride, and even went so far as to go as Jimmy Durante one Halloween, but no teenage girl likes overhearing herself described as "Toucan Sam." Your parents couldn't afford to fix it, but you've been saving, and you finally have enough to get a good old-fashioned nose job. Your mother always said your nose gave you character—but screw character. You want attention from *boys.*

Two Weeks Later

The swelling has gone down, and you look wonderful. Now you can go to Lutheran potlucks without people asking you when you converted.

Four Weeks Later

You're enjoying an Aviation at the local bar when your ex-boyfriend Darryl shows up. He starts talking to you, and it quickly becomes clear he doesn't recognize you at all—a good thing, considering how you treated him. You have the presence of mind to introduce yourself with a fake name, and seize the chance to try again with The One That Got Away. Now that the oxygen has a shorter route to your brain, maybe you'll manage to be less of a bitch.

Four Months Later

Wow. Darryl is a successful patent attorney, a solid B+ in the sack, and that unpleasant mother of his died while you were split. You don't know how you were ever so cruel—so *foolish*—as to refer to him as "a boring little tan belt man." He may not be Evel Knievel, but he's a good provider. You're ready to cut your past loose and wife it up with Darryl. He need never know this is Round Two.

Four Years Later

Marriage agrees with you. You feel happy and at peace as you watch Darryl play with your son, and you smile as you run your hand over your pregnant belly.

Four Years, Three Months Later

Disaster. You give birth to a healthy baby girl . . . with a nose the size of an adult's fist. It makes the nurses uneasy.

Twenty Years Later

Your daughter's nose has torn your family apart. As she grew into a young woman, she began to look exactly like you had before your surgery. You began to notice things—little things, but telling. Darryl never asks about her when he calls from a business trip, and you notice he sometimes flinches when she speaks to him. Once, drunk after a Christmas party, he told you how eerie, how uncanny it is that his own daughter should look so much like the woman who tried to destroy him so many years ago.

Twenty-Three Years Later

Sensing her father's horror, your daughter ran off with some idiot on a motorcycle, only to return a few months later filled with shame . . . and a fetus. As she gives birth, you steel yourself to face what you know it will be: a healthy baby girl—with a honker like an anteater.

Get a Tattoo

When you find yourself separated from the rest of your brother's bachelor party, aimlessly wandering the boardwalk with mom's bankcard and more Malibu in your bloodstream than platelets, pretty much *everything* seems like a good idea. Riding the Haunted Ghost Train until you vomit? Yes. Paying cash to have "Give me head 'til I'm dead" airbrushed on an otherwise perfectly good T-shirt? God yes. Feeling up a girl you just met on a dance floor to the beat of Cascada's "Every Time We Touch" and then "bouncing"? Frankly, We're disappointed you didn't think of it sooner. But you know what would be a really, *really* good idea? Getting a tattoo. You've always wanted one and the shops are still open, so now that you've gotten your drink on, get your ink on.

Five Minutes Later

God, why do *all* Aerosmith song lyrics have to be so perfectly perfect? You'd rather choose a favorite child than a favorite line from "Janie's Got a Gun," so you decide to peruse the shop's extensive wall of flash art instead.

Forty-Five Minutes Later

Irritated by your own indecisiveness, you close your eyes, point to a random spot on the wall and land on what looks to you like a set of crosshairs. You decide the design is actually perfect because it's like, you're always in like, *life's* crosshairs, you know?

Two Days Later

You upload a picture of you sporting your new ink to your Facebook account.

Two Days and Ten Minutes Later

Four hundred thirty-six angry Facebook comments and a quick Google search can't be wrong: your new tattoo isn't of a set of crosshairs—it's Odin's Cross, the international symbol for white power.

One Month Later

You make an appointment with the dermatologist to have the tattoo removed. After the procedure, he shakes your hand, tells you he thinks you're a fine young man and gives you a number to call. You call the number and it turns out to belong to a TV producer who's developing a Katie Couric special about people leaving hate groups, tentatively titled "Leaving the Hate." You agree to do it in hopes that they'll reimburse you for the tattoo removal, which was surprisingly expensive.

Two Months Later

The special airs and is so popular that you become a fixture on the high school inspirational lecture circuit.

Six Months Later

After a picture of you shaking hands with President Obama and Al Sharpton in the White House Rose Garden lands on the cover of *Newsweek*, a journalist uncovers your Facebook announcement titled "I THOUGHT IT WAS CROSSHAIRS AND MY BEST FRIEND IS PART CHEROKEE" and your story is blown.

One Year Later

Now addicted to the limelight and unable to land any more lecturing gigs, you and James Frey go on the road with a vaudeville-style revue called "Lies and Laffs!"

 **Take a Yoga Class**

It's a new year and this one is going to be different. This year you're going to finally take control of your life and become the vibrant, sophisticated not-wearing-sweatpants-to-happy-hour woman that you always knew you could be. Gone are the days when you'd pay a $15 delivery charge on an $8 order of sweet and sour pork because you didn't want to put a bra on and go down the street to get it. No longer will you refer to that oversized Umbro shirt as your "nightgown," and from now on you won't pee in the shower unless you're in a hurry or really hungover. Because you're better than all of that! Or at least you will be after a little low-impact yoga at the nearby studio. Starting off slow is always a good idea and maybe if you get your chakras aligned you'll finally have enough energy to do laundry instead of ordering fresh pairs of underwear on Amazon every two weeks. After spending $75 on an assortment of eco-friendly sweatbands and a pair of ill-fitting pants, you're ready to hit the mat.

Thirty Minutes Later

As Guru Dan spots your shaky attempt to assume the Distressed Mantis position, you're surprised at how much you're enjoying yourself.

One Month Later

Under Guru Dan's caring tutelage, you've mastered a number of advanced positions, including The Anxious Camel, The Pensive Seahorse, and The Confused Lemur. You start taking classes five days a week instead of two.

Three Months Later

Yoga has really turned your life around. You've completely connected to your inner self and while you don't consider yourself religious, you do consider yourself to be *spiritual*.

Six Months Later

You find that the energy coming from your collection of crystals is really speeding along the healing process of your new lotus flower tattoo.

Eight Months Later

You now exclusively say "namaste" instead of hello, goodbye, thank you, and excuse me. It's like aloha but more pretentious.

Eleven Months Later

Thanksgiving was a disaster ("I was *told* there would be a tofurkey . . .") and you ruin dinner party conversations talking about the sacred orgasms you've been having during tantric sex with your partner.

Two Years Later

As the sun sets over Marin County, you and your new yogi, Jeremy Piven, toast the cosmic oneness with champagne flutes filled with gently carbonated organic fair-trade wheat grass juice. You feel so lucky to be part of his Nirvantourage.

Seventy-Four Years Later

From your perspective, nothing bad happened to you, but everyone else found you insufferable for the rest of your life. Privately, even Jeremy Piven fantasized about yanking out one of your dangly little Om sign earrings, officially making you the Turtle of the group.

Grow an Ironic Moustache

Looking down at your cargo pants and sensible man sandals, it's hard to believe that you were once the epitome of hip. True, you were the epitome of hip back in 1992 when all it took was a braided rattail and a Jansport backpack artfully slung over one shoulder, but a moment of glory is a moment of glory. You have it on good authority from your nephew, Jed, that moustaches are what's "happening" with the "kids," and considering he lives in Pittsburgh and wears a fedora, you're apt to believe him. You immediately stop shaving your upper lip and are ready for the cool points to be accredited to your account.

One Week Later
The mustache isn't growing in quite as quickly as you thought it would. You look less like Tom Selleck and more like the teenager other teenagers think looks old enough to buy beer.

Two Weeks Later
It's filling out more and more every day, but you decide to hang on to those *Male Hormone Levels: A Balancing Act* pamphlets the doctor gave you just in case.

Three Weeks Later
Your patience has paid off—you finally have a bona fide, tightly trimmed, well-kept little lip tickler.

One Month Later
Although you love your moustache (you've named him "Steve" and make a point to brush him a hundred times with the rake from your desktop Zen garden every night before bed), the rest of the world seems

to feel differently. It feels like you get angry stares everywhere you go and even your friends have started to hang out with you less and less. You chalk it up to 'stache envy and reassure Steve that it's not his fault.

Six Weeks Later

Your boss inexplicably takes you off the Rosenthal account and tells you to "cool your jets" in the mailroom.

Seven Weeks Later

A large, aggressive-looking bald-headed man approaches you in the subway and shakes your hand. "Thank you," he says, with an almost startling level of sincerity. You ask him what for and he simply whispers, "For your *courage*," and aggressively points to something just behind you.

Two Months Later

Confused, you approach Jed at a family gathering and ask him if this kind of reaction is normal. Jed looks thoughtful for a moment, puts one hand on your shoulder, and gently explains that because of your natural salt and pepper hair coloring, your moustache has grown in white on the sides and jet black in the middle. "Right, like a calico cat," you say. "No, like Hitler," he clarifies.

Two Months and One Hour Later

Jed loans you his straight razor and you blitz Steve right off.

Enter a Beauty Pageant

In retrospect, getting your masters degree in Medieval European History was probably a bad decision. True, it kept you from having to find a job for two years and you got to live out your ultimate (and oddly attainable) fantasy of being a TA, but it's left you $30,000 in debt without a single job prospect. Inspired by your stepsister's recent blue-ribbon finish at the Lil' Miss Baldwin County Agriculture and Industry Pageant, you've decided to enter a beauty pageant yourself for a chance at some prize money.

One Day Later

You run into your first roadblock when you find out that the cutoff age for the Miss South Alabama Subaru Pageant is eighteen years old. Never one to give up (like a true south Alabama beauty), you fashion a set of makeshift braces out of two paperclips and a stick of Trident, overtweeze your eyebrows, and get a fake ID. You are seventeen again.

Two Days Later

They fell for your ruse and you are an official contestant at the Miss South Alabama Subaru Pageant at the Dothan Comfort Inn.

Two Weeks Later

As the day of the pageant draws closer, it dawns on you that unless writing a twenty-page essay about Blanche of Castile's exercise of royal power during the crusades is something you can use for the talent portion, you need a new trick. You lock yourself in the garage and teach yourself how to play the theme song from *Gone with the Wind* on a musical saw with the help of a series of YouTube videos and you're back in the pageant.

One Month Later

It's the day of the competition and you're feeling ready. You've managed to squeeze yourself into your Junior Prom dress (a Dillard's original), you've tuned your musical saw, and applied a fresh coat of Vaseline to your teeth to encourage smiling. You survey your competition and your only serious threat is a blonde-haired, blue-eyed scoliosis victim from Birmingham whose talents are playing Toby Keith's "Courtesy of the Red, White, and Blue (The Angry American)" on the harp and overcoming adversity.

One Month and Thirty Minutes Later

As God is our witness, no one will ever play the *Gone with the Wind* theme song on a musical saw that well again.

One Month and One Hour Later

You're crowned runner-up behind the blonde shoo-in. You missed out on the $10,000 cash, instead winning a two-year scholarship to Chattahoochee Valley Community College, in lovely Phoenix City, Alabama, for the program of your choice. You consider walking away in disgust, but a thought strikes you . . .

Two Years Later

You've just gotten an associate's degree in medical billing. It took you the better part of a decade, but you're finally employable.

Get a Spa Treatment

Your sister has been understandably depressed recently, what with her recent breakup, sudden layoff, and totaling her '01 Acura Legend. You decide to do the sisterly thing and take her out for a spa day, just you gals. While perusing the menu on the spa's website, you see a great massage/rose water soak/sauna package for two and book it for you and your sister. The next day you pick her up and take her to the spa for a ladies' day of luxury.

Thirty Minutes Later

You check in at the spa, change into robes, and wait to be taken to your respective spa rooms. To your surprise, the attendant leads you both to the same dimly lit room with sensual saxophone music playing in the background and two petal-strewn massage tables a sensual hand's hold distance apart. It slowly sinks in that you inadvertently purchased a couple's spa package, which you probably should have gathered from the flowery script and liberal usage of "amour" in the description. While the masseuses are preparing the equipment, you and your sister consult and decide to just go with it. People with totaled Acuras can't be choosers.

One Hour and Thirty Minutes Later

With your sensual massages over, the spa attendant leads you to your next treatment—a rose water soak in an oversized heart shape bathtub. You spend the entire time talking about your favorite architects, avoiding eye contact, and desperately making sure your legs don't touch.

Two Hours Later

Now in the sauna, you're naked and sweaty with your sister, who everyone thinks is your lesbian lover. You've never been *more* uncomfortable . . .

Two Hours and Thirty Minutes Later

You think you're done, but as you hurriedly pay and turn to leave, the cashier says, "You're such an adorable couple! Let's see a kiss!" and the overly supportive staff begins to chant, "KISS! KISS! KISS!" The path of least resistance seems to be the way out of here. You give your sister a woodpecker-like smackaroo and bolt out the door. The car ride home is *intensely* silent.

One Week Later

You go out for drinks and spend the entire evening not mentioning the spa and talking about current events in high, unnatural voices.

Three Years Later

You're asked to step in at the last moment as your sister's birth videographer. Her husband never understands why you kept the camera trained on her face the entire time.

Ten Years Later

You have a breast cancer scare but don't want to tell her because you're too bashful to say "breast" in front of her.

Fifteen Years Later

At your mother's funeral, you and your sister comfort each other with a brisk, arms-length hug. It's still awkward.

Do an At-Home Face Mask

You're willing to endure a painful situation, provided there's a good enough reason. That four-hour-long session at the tattoo shop was *far* from pleasant, but an Allman Brothers back piece is forever. And that mole removal was no day at the beach, but when you're talking about irregular borders, better be safe than sorry. A professional facial, however, doesn't seem worth the pain. Not only does it hurt when they dig in with the pore scraper, it becomes mentally exhausting when the Russian esthetician yells at you in broken English about how you need to drink more water and take a B vitamin because you look "all papery." You decide to save yourself some time and trouble and freshen your face with an at-home face mask. Maybe you can peel it off in one whole piece and frighten the dog!

One Hour Later

You drive to Sally Beauty Supply and survey your face mask options: seaweed scrub, honey almond peel, cucumber and cilantro dip 'n' dab (as good on a chip as it is on your face). In the end, you decide to go with a solid, straightforward detoxifying mud mask and pick up some Jolen Creme Bleach for touch-ups while you're there.

Two Hours Later

Once home, you put on your robe, pour a glass of Kendall-Jackson Pinot Noir, light a Drift Away–scented Yankee Candle, turn on the Sade, slather on the mud, and let the beauty soak in.

Ten Hours Later

You awake with a start. You didn't mean to go to sleep, but the combination of Drift Away, Sade, and Kendall-Jackson strong-armed you into dreamland. You're on the verge of being late for work, so you quickly dress, pausing only to slap on a coat of red lipstick before you head out the door.

Ten Hours and Thirty Minutes Later

You know you didn't take much time on your hair this morning, but do people really need to glare at you over it? You've seen people eat mashed potatoes with their *hands* on the bus; surely they can forgive a few flyaways.

Eleven Hours Later

You breeze into the office with minutes to spare. You smile at Keisha, the receptionist, on the way in. She fixes you with a startled look and murmurs, "We've still got a *long* way to go." I guess she's still annoyed that you forgot her birthday.

Eleven Hours and Ten Minutes Later

You reach your desk and sit down. As you turn toward your computer to switch it on, you catch a reflection of yourself in the monitor. It seems you forgot to wash the mud off as you hurried out the door this morning; that effect, coupled with the lipstick, means you inadvertently went to work in blackface. You wear an Obama '12 T-shirt the next day, but it doesn't seem to help.

Become a Vegan

You went to a Sleater-Kinney reunion concert to meet girls, and you were *not* disappointed. Because it was there that you met her—the girl of your dreams. She walked up to you in all of her American Apparel–legginged glory and asked if you had a moment for animal rights. You'd have a moment for the *Taliban* for this broad. Hoping to score points, you lied and told her you were a vegan already, but are always looking for ways to make your life more cruelty-free. One thing led to another, and before you knew it, you had a vegan girlfriend and were eating corn dogs in the crawl space in the attic to get your meat fix. It may not be a good idea to start a relationship based on lies, but, frankly, dat ass just won't quit.

One Week Later

You choke down the bok choy with lentil sauce your girlfriend made for dinner and make an excuse to leave. You put on a fedora, trench coat, and sunglasses, drive to a nearby town, and get a mega burger with pork fries.

Two Weeks Later

Gas money to drive thirty miles for a mega burger is eating you alive. You decide it will be ultimately cheaper to try to
get used to vegan food.

Three Weeks Later

While trying to concoct better-tasting vegan food in your kitchen, you discover that you have quite a knack for meat-free cooking. Every dish you bring to the freaky vegan potlucks your girlfriend makes you attend, are a hit. "It's like my teeth are *actually* tearing through the flesh of a defensive animal!"

Two Months Later

You decide to start a vegan food truck called "Helen of Soy" and it's a hit with the downtown working crowd.

One Year Later

You expand Helen of Soy into a sit-down, casual dining establishment. The food critic at *Time Out Chicago* hails it as, "Pitch perfect! It launches a thousand ships of flavor!"

One Year and Two Months Later

Word of your culinary prowess reaches Bobby Flay, who, upon hearing that there's a talented chef who's not Bobby Flay, throws a temper tantrum, soils himself, and vows to get his revenge.

One Year, Two Months and One Week Later

While glazing the top of a delightful little vegan crème brûlée, Bobby Flay unexpectedly bursts through the wall of your kitchen with a camera crew and declares that he's challenging you to a vegan entrée throwdown. You accept, and ultimately defeat his soy lobster thermidor with your no-nonsense whey and protein pigs in a blanket. Defeated, Flay reverts to his true leprechaun form and must grant you a wish. You wish that your girlfriend just ate meat and you could put an end to all this madness and he begrudgingly complies.

One Year, Two Months, One Week, and Two Hours Later

You arrive home to find your girlfriend on the sofa, naked, and eating an entire ham. God bless America!

Participate in a Medical Trial

If you've said it once, you've said it a thousand times: you didn't know the gun was loaded. You assumed people budgeted for hunting accidents, but apparently not, and long story short, here you are with a whole *heap* of court costs to pay. You've started to think outside the box for how you can pay your legal fees. You considered stripping, but you're about fifteen pounds and a third nipple away from being stage ready. You thought about selling the Beanie Baby you bought in 1997 as an investment, but it turns out Stephanie the Stick Insect's appeal is limited. While flipping through the local free paper, you saw an ad seeking women ages eighteen to forty-five for a clinical trial. You may not have much, but you have a body and most of it works! You call the number, set up an appointment, and hope the compensation covers a day's worth of litigation.

One Day Later

The evening before your appointment, you stand nude in front of the mirror, and explore your complex feelings about your body.

Two Days Later

You arrive at the clinic and are told the trial is to test the safety and efficacy of a new radium-coated contraceptive IUD, CerviGlo®. At least it doesn't go in your butt.

Six Weeks Later

You have your CerviGlo® removed and get your check for $5,550, plus $65 merit pay for being a good sport. The only side effects you noticed were a tingling in your stomach and a light flush in your cheeks . . . but maybe you're just in love?

Six Months Later

You go back to the clinic for a follow-up and receive some upsetting news: the radium coating rubbed off in your uterus, leaving it moderately radioactive. The doctor advises you it would be unsafe to have children because, "There's a 1 percent chance they'll be a superhero and a 99 percent chance they'll come out looking like a Cubist painting."

Eight Years Later

You Google "infertility solutions" and the 13,976th result is monkid .org, a website that allows you to adopt a monkey as a surrogate child. It seems considerably easier than human adoption, so you go for it.

Fifteen Years Later

Your monkid, now a teenager, has been acting out recently. Once upon a time he was a cuddly little primate in footy pajamas clinging to mama's leg, and now he's stealing smokes from his grandmother and throwing feces at you when you tell him to clean his room. You hate to do it, but it seems like the only answer is military school.

Fifteen Years and Three Months Later

The day before Thanksgiving, you go to the bus depot to pick up your monkid, who's coming home for the holiday. He gets off the bus with his head held high, walks up to you, puts down his bags, and gives you a firm, respectful handshake. Tears well up in your eyes as you realize, your troubled monkid has become a fine, young monkman.

Pop a Zit

You felt heavier when you woke up this morning, so you got out of bed, went into the bathroom, and got on the scale. You looked down at the number, "Nope, still 120 reasons to love me!" Relieved, you stepped off, turned toward the mirror and saw the culprit—it's the biggest zit on your face you have ever seen since hitting puberty. It's a *doozy*. You know you're not supposed to, but every inch of your being is telling you to pop that sucker and nip it in the bud. There's really no classy way to describe popping a zit, but you do it. It looks a little better, so you slather on your concealer and go about your day.

One Day Later

You wake up and even before you get out of bed, you know it's gotten worse. The entire right side of your face is hot and throbbing. You sit in front of a magnified mirror and just what your mother said would happen did: you popped a zit and it got more infected. Now *no* boy is going to want to go with you to the Sadie Hawkins dance!

One Day and Twelve Hours Later

Archie dumps you for Veronica and you're left at the clambake all alone.

Two Days Later

During a nuclear strike drill, Bobby Thomas won't cower under the same desk as you because, in his words, "Anyone with a face that red *has* to be a commie!"

Two Days and Three Hours Later

Jeepers! It *would* be cheerleader tryouts today!

Two Days and Eight Hours Later

That night at dinner, your father gives you the once over and remarks, "Not gonna get your MRS with that Z-I-T, are ya kitten." *"Hank!"* your mother scolds. "Oh, I'm just funnin' her, Jane, he replies. She knows she's my baby girl, don't ya darlin'?"

Two Days and Ten Hours Later

You borrow daddy's T-Bird and go to the drive-in to take your mind off your stressful day. When the ten-foot sea monster takes over the screen, Ralph Cooper, in his father's shiny new Ford Galaxie, shouts, "Hey! That looks like Sally Miller's huge zit!" As the crowd laughs, you put on your sunglasses, tie a scarf over your hair, and slump down in the seat.

Two Days and Thirteen Hours Later

Your mother knocks softly on your bedroom door and then enters. "I went to the drugstore earlier and I think you and I should have a little talk," she says. You hope she doesn't want to bring up your P-E-R-I-O-D again, but instead she pulls out a white tube and hands it to you with a wink. "It's a little medicine that should clear up your 'big' problem," she says. "Why, I used Clearasil when I was a girl!" You applied a coat before bed and when you woke up, the P-I-M-P-L-E was gone! Thanks, Mom! You vow to remember that clean teens always use Clearasil.

Have a Good Cry

Every now and then, you just need to have a good cry. It doesn't make you less of a man; in fact it makes you more of one, because real men have feelings. Nothing is more cathartic than putting on a pair of sweats, assuming the fetal position on the sofa, breaking out the good tissues with aloe, watching that Humane Society commercial with Sarah McLachlan, and bursting into loud, wracking, unashamed sobs. The problem is, you've done this so often that you've developed a resistance to the commercial and even the collie with one eye can't bring you to tears. It's time to find something else to make you cry and release the tension before it builds up and gives you diarrhea again.

One Day Later

You watch the *Golden Girls* episode where Blanche dreams her husband is still alive and then wakes up, alone and confused, reaching out for George, but finding only an empty spot on the other side of the bed. It reminds you that Betty White is on Letterman tonight, so you're more excited than tearful.

Two Days Later

You try listening to Toni Braxton's "Unbreak My Heart" for a few hours. You can't remember if she has lupus or sickle cell anemia, so you do a quick check on Wikipedia. Four hours later, you realize you're reading about Christmas Island when you should be crying.

Three Days Later

You call your father to talk about how his drug use affected you when you were younger, hoping it'll lead you to a screaming fight that will bring you to tears. Instead, he apologizes and offers to send you money to come visit him in Arizona, "when you're ready."

Four Days Later

You start looking at a picture of you with your first girlfriend, Helena. Remember how much fun you had? How much you loved her? And how great her tits were . . . ? You wind up finding some "relief" while looking at the picture, but not quite what you were after.

Five Days Later

You've tried to avoid this, but it's time for the big guns. You pull out your battered VHS of *Charlotte's Web*, watch it, and are immediately wracked with convulsive sobs.

Six Days Later

You find a spider in the corner of your bedroom. You decide to gently scoop her up and transfer her outside so she can live free, but it seems you've misread her body language, and she feels threatened and bites you. You suffer an allergic reaction from the venom and as you lie gasping to death on the floor, you take comfort in the fact that Helena will probably come to the funeral, and if you're lucky, might even rest her boobs on your coffin as she says goodbye.

Get a Flu Shot

You consider yourself a pretty healthy person. You take a Centrum Women's multivitamin every morning with a glass of orange juice, walk to work, and always make sure to carry a little thing of key-lime-and-mango-scented hand sanitizer with you wherever you go. As a result of this healthy lifestyle, you don't really get sick that often, but when your company started giving out free flu shots, you were first in line. You wanted the shot for the same reason you're always the one to take home the leftover breakfast pastries after meetings—you like free shit. You have a T-shirt from every convention you've ever been to and stayed with the same dry cleaner that shrunk your wedding dress because he gives a free desk calendar every year at Christmas. If anyone's handing out free anything, even if it's a dose of dead or inactivated virus, you'll take one. Two if they'll let you.

Fifteen Minutes Later

You're disappointed when the flu shot technician doesn't give you free donuts and orange juice, but then remember that's for giving blood. Maybe the Red Cross will be around again soon.

Two Weeks Later

You've been holed up with the flu for two weeks despite having had the flu shot. Confused, you go online to research what could have gone wrong and discover a burgeoning web community of conspiracy theorists who think the government is trying to thin out the population by giving them so-called "flu shots" that instead make them ill. Maybe it's the fever, but they're making a lot of sense to you.

Two Months Later

Your body is back to normal but your sense of outrage is not. Dedicated to exposing the truth, you anonymously contact reporters across the country hoping they'll pick up the story. Only one does: a newly minted Northwestern journalism grad working the city beat at the *Sacramento Bee*. He's got everything to prove and nothing to lose.

Six Months Later

Working in tandem with the journalist and a secret congressional contact, you find that this one goes all the way to the top. You have a storage unit full of evidence. You contact a freshman senator who ran on a platform of transparency and good government, and he arranges for you to address Congress.

Seven Months Later

Once confronted with the damning public evidence, the government's lies start to fold like a house of cards. Realizing that honesty is their only chance to avert widespread unrest, the government admits to the flu shot conspiracy as well as the truth about Area 51, the truth about the Kennedy assassination, and the truth about what *actually* happened between Monica and Bill. John Q. Taxpayer is better informed . . . but is he happier?

CHAPTER 2

Oh, the Places You'll Blow!

Going Where You Shouldn't Have Gone

Here's a riddle. What do these two people have in common: an atheist at a Creed concert and the chubbiest girl at cheerleader camp? Answer: the same thought cuts through each mind—"Wow, I *really* should not have come here." Agoraphobics face their own challenges, but they're never caught in the cross-fire when a well-meaning flash mob turns into a good old-fashioned riot. Before going anywhere, even down to the corner for smokes, make sure you carefully evaluate who will be there, how flammable the structure is, and what escape routes you will have—because you never know what might happen. Forewarned is forearmed.

A Hurricane Party

Your fascination with severe weather has cost you a few relationships. It turns out that "epic" is not how your Louisiana-born ex-girlfriend remembers Katrina, and while your Oklahoman kickboxing instructor does get homesick, it's not because F-5 tornadoes are "frickin' sweet." You don't want to seem callous—you understand that lives are lost and property destroyed in these events—but you can't get over your burning desire to see a disaster from the inside. You're in luck this summer: no sooner did you arrive on the scenic Caribbean island of St. Genevieve, off the coast of Puerto Rico, than the weather service announced that Hurricane Rhonda, a sassy little Category 4, was on her way and had something to prove. The resort staff tried to evacuate you, but you waved them away. You and a few other brave souls would stay, raid the mini-bars, and have a good old-fashioned hurricane party. As the storm bears down, you suck down a few miniature bottles of rum and get ready to *finally* see what all the fuss is about.

Two Hours Later

Well, here you are, throwing up Captain Morgan and bile on the carpet in the middle of a hurricane. Your last thought is a vague hope that the vomit stain will blend in with the pattern and the hotel staff won't see it and keep your deposit.

Eight Hours Later

You wake up, having missed most of the hurricane while you were passed out. You stagger outside to check what's what, and see that most of the resort and surrounding area is badly damaged. The other guests who stayed are crowded around a battery-operated radio. An announcer is saying that due to the severity of the storm rescue efforts are not to be expected for several days.

Two Weeks Later

Your little band of travelers have eaten all the Hot Pockets and drunk all the rum, so you're trying to make fishing gear out of plants. Before the last set of batteries craps out, you hear from the radio that FEMA has elected not to search for survivors, citing hazardous conditions, "not really feeling like it," and a preference for watching Valerie Harper on *Dancing with the Stars*.

One Year Later

You and the other survivors have built a primitive society. You have two wives, a well-thatched hut, and an ample preserve of dried fish set aside for winter. After the storm, you all developed an aversion to water, and only go to the coast to fish. A search party finally arrived several moons ago, but for reasons you didn't fully understand, you and the tribe hid from them. You feel they wouldn't understand you now.

Fifty Years Later

As the younger tribesmen lash you to a rock and prepare to cut out your heart as a sacrifice to appease the eternally hungering ocean goddess T'Katl, you reflect that you probably should have gotten your hurricane fix by riding a carnival Tilt-a-Whirl on a rainy day.

Into the Wild

Camping, especially alone, really lets you get in tune with yourself. Several days of solitude, with only nature for company, focuses the mind, cleanses the soul, and frees a man to consider what truly matters. When camping, you join Darwin, Thoreau, and countless other thinkers inspired by nature in the contemplation of our planetary home, this natural realm that mankind depends upon even as he corrupts it. Finally, at the close of each day as the sunset gradually burns away to reveal the starry jewels of the night sky, you gaze at your campfire and ponder the eternal question: "If I pound another Natty Light, can I extinguish this fire using only my own urine?" You are truly at one with the outdoors.

Five Minutes Later

As you aim your "hose" at the base of the fire, you notice an odd light on the horizon. The fire hisses, gutters, and goes out while the light seems to grow larger, brighter, and somehow nearer. Suddenly the light becomes blinding and you hear a loud "whoosh!" that seems to come from everywhere at once.

Ten Minutes Later

Judging from the view out the windows, the complex navigational equipment, and the seven-foot-tall blue lizardlike beings chittering excitedly, you would guess that you have been abducted onto an alien spacecraft. With surprising gentleness, they lead you to a small room that appears to be your new quarters; cramped, dingy, and full of back issues of *Maxim*, it reminds you of your freshman dorm room.

Two Days Later

The good news: they've abducted a woman for you to mate with. The weird news: it's Charo. The good news: she's kind of into it.

Seven Days Later

The aliens treat you as a pet, energetically rubbing you behind the ears when you amuse them and cuddling you when they feel sad. It's a little demeaning, but they keep your dish full.

Three Weeks Later

Your spaceship takes part in the climactic Battle of the Red Nebula, a desperate attempt to prevent the Quaxi'i Pirates from breaking through the Republic's defensive embargo. None of the blue lizards laugh when you say, "He's dead, Jim."

Six Weeks Later

If no one's going to pay attention to you, you're just going to crap in someone's shoes and see if they can ignore you *then*. Shouting ensues, and you are unceremoniously dumped back on Earth near where you were abducted.

Twelve Weeks Later

No one believes your story, but it is vivid enough to get you on an episode of *Maury*. The audience was fairly rude, but the $300 you earned is enough to get you to Las Vegas and see if things with Charo might lead somewhere.

Fourteen Weeks Later

Charo thinks you're a nice boy, but needs to focus on her career.

A Study Abroad Program

Yikes. You should really begin concentrating on your studies more—a 2.07 GPA isn't going to impress anyone other than your fraternity brothers, who tend to skate along at around 1.8. You have to find a way to get better grades without cutting back on your drinking or skirt chasing. As you ponder this, you notice a flyer announcing your school's study abroad program. "All classes will be graded pass/fail—your GPA will be unchanged, but your education will be immeasurably enriched." Also, Italian chicks. You are *in*.

Four Months Later

You've taken a picture of yourself "holding up" the Leaning Tower of Pisa, given one of the Vatican Swiss Guards a wedgie, and vomited some "gently used" Chianti into a Venetian canal. No one can say you haven't had the American Student in Italy Experience. You really have enjoyed it here, so you decide to do a little more traveling.

Five Months Later

Only forty euros to ride a donkey down the Albanian coast? What a steal!

Six Months Later

You've spent the last two weeks in Istanbul meeting "the real people," which in this case means playing the hostel's PlayStation with a rotating cast of drunk English girls and Germans with rebellious hairstyles and ostentatiously awful table manners. Everyone agrees you're very good at Tomb Raider "for an American."

Seven Months Later

It turns out the cheapest way to get from here to there is to fly standby to Oman and then see if anyone will take you across on a fishing boat. It's a little wild, but life is a journey, you know?

Nine Months Later

You leave Thailand in a huff because it's full of Westerners. It's not *really* Asia, not anymore.

Eleven Months Later

Hiking through northeastern China, you decide to take a swim in the river you've been walking along, so you strip down to the buff and dive in. Boy, are you surprised when a group of policemen from the other side of the river dive in, seize you, and drag you back. Turns out that was the Yalu River, and you are probably the first American to be arrested for skinny-dipping in North Korean Territorial Waters.

Fourteen Months Later

You could stand the beatings, sleep deprivation, and even the waterboarding, but the documentaries about the "glorious leader" and his magical urine that irrigates a million acres of wheat are wearing you down. After each of these, your captors present you with a lump of tofu formed into the shape of Bill Clinton's head and order you to "defile your leader with your hunger." They're a little behind.

Eighteen Months Later

You've made so much progress that you get to be in the Yongaepaerong Political Instruction Performance Games! You will dance as part of the Great Leader's shirt collar during the Portrait Dance. You are pleased to do this for the leader, who is like a father and mother to you. You don't think he looks like he has a hormone imbalance at *all*.

Mini-Golfing

You know what adults don't do enough? Just have fun. Sure, people go on wine tours or have affairs or grow heirloom tomatoes, but so rarely do grownups spontaneously go out and do something silly or whimsical purely for the purpose of enjoying themselves. No longer. You are going to reclaim "fun" for your generation, starting with a good old-fashioned round of miniature golf.

Five Minutes Later

Hole 2 is a par 3. Two mulligans and one "I was just practicing" later, you take a 7 for the hole and move on. This is more frustrating than you expected.

Ten Minutes Later

Hole 5 is a windmill hole. You hit a blade on four consecutive tries, sending the ball back past the tee and provoking a strange anti-Dutch rant culminating in the phrase, "I'll wind *your* mills, you dike-building sadists!"

Fifteen Minutes Later

Hole 7: "Dinosaur Alley." You're going to be adult about this. You take your time, line up your shot carefully, make sure your grip is right, make sure your hips aren't locked, keep your eye on the hole, follow through, and send the ball right into the tyrannosaurus' mouth.

Twenty-Five Minutes Later

At Hole 12, you're so frustrated by your obvious incompetence at miniature golf that you rear up, put your back into it, and absolutely whack the snot out of the ball. It caroms off the edge of the ramp and goes flying, banks off a plaster replica of the Arc de Triomphe, and falls in a little ornamental wishing well. Furious with yourself, the concept of miniature golf, the Hispanic family who's pointing and laughing at you, and the son of a bitch who invented wells, you march over to reclaim your ball. The well is deeper than it appears from the outside, and before you know it you've overbalanced, slipped, and stuck yourself headfirst into the well. You think this is the most humiliating thing to ever happen to you, but then you feel a cool breeze as your skirt gently wafts down and settles around your waist.

Four Hours Later

As you're sitting on the couch sulking and watching the news, Dan Yakori, Metro 7's perfectly coiffed anchorman, announces, "Now on the *lighter* side—ever wonder what would have happened if Baby Jessica had grown up to have an anger management problem, swear like a trucker, and wear lacy thongs? The Gonzales family of Arvada found out *exactly* what that would look like at the Putt and Play today. Their footage—when we return."

The Open Ocean

Bonding activities with your father always seem to backfire. When he took you hunting, you managed to injure—but not kill—the deer, and then in a sobbing panic you ran forward and tried to club it to death with the butt of your rifle. On your eighteenth birthday, he took you to be "initiated" by a lady of the evening—you wound up dating her and paying for her night class, but still not getting any. To forestall another awkward weekend, you've decided to teach yourself to fish. It may be the least manly of the manly pursuits, but beggars can't be choosers, and hopefully he'll appreciate the fact that you actually touched a worm.

One Hour Later

You're out on the charter boat, Dramamine and sunblock still holding firm. You drop your line into the water and almost immediately catch an enormous fish that takes a good ten minutes to reel in.

Four Hours Later

You only manage to catch that one fish, but she's a beaut! After returning to the marina, you have your picture with the fish made before dropping it off to be stuffed.

One Day Later

You mail the picture of you with your prize fish to your father. Won't he be proud!

Four Days Later

He is not proud. According to your father's reply, that fish you caught is a specimen of the absurdly endangered South Atlantic orange-flanked dory, "which you would know if you'd paid attention in the marine life unit of Boy Scouts instead of diddling yourself."

One Week Later

Wracked with guilt, you go back out where you caught the fish and try to safely capture a breeding pair. Maybe you can save these beautiful angels of the sea!

Two Years Later

Your house is full of tanks containing healthy, happy, hearty South Atlantic orange-flanked dories. Your special pet is Clementine—granted, you can't really tell the sex of the fishes, but she has a certain feminine elegance.

Three Years Later

Things with Clementine are going *swimmingly*. You realize now that it's foolish to assume that true love can exist only between members of the same species—how shallow! (Get it?) An open-minded notary with an online ordination agrees to bind you to Clementine forever—your dad's pissed, but for once you don't care.

Three Years, One Week Later

Michelle Bachmann's white paper entitled "See, They're Marrying Fish Now" is faxed to every statehouse in the country. The gay marriage movement is dealt a crippling blow from which it never recovers, since apparently if you give people an inch they'll take a (nautical) mile.

An Amusement Park

You guess some adults would spend a three-day weekend thinking about their investment portfolios and watching *Masterpiece Mystery*, but not you. You and your friends have decided to go to the amusement park for a day of funnel cake, roller coasters, and failed seductions of costumed cartoon characters. It may not be the most mature decision or the wisest use of a day off, but that "buy one, get one free" admission coupon you got on a can of Sprite isn't going to redeem itself.

One Hour Later

You all decide to have one of those sepia-toned wild west photographs made, but it ends in tears when there aren't enough saloon girl dresses to go around and you have to be the sheriff.

Two Hours Later

You get your funnel cake, but the potent combination of sugar and oil makes your blood glucose spike—and crash. You have to lie down in the medical tent for a while and drink some water.

Three Hours Later

You neglect to take your keys out of your pocket before going down the Lazy River. They pierce your inner tube, and it sends you whizzing wildly down the river as it deflates.

Four Hours Later

You elect to ride a roller coaster to try to dry yourself off after your not-so-Lazy River experience. You enjoy the ride, and after it's over stop by to see the picture of you taken by the automatic camera at the first drop. You're amazed. The sudden downward acceleration has pulled your jowls up and back, making your face look elegantly thin. You buy the most lavish set of prints there is.

One Week Later

You return to the amusement park wearing a nice dress, hoping to get some good skinny pictures to use on match.com. These work out so well you return in a business suit for your work picture, in a reindeer sweater for your Christmas card picture, and in a sequined gown with your high school boyfriend to replace your unflattering pictures.

One Year Later

The *Guinness Book of World Records* contacts you. Apparently, you've ridden the roller coaster so many times trying to get good pictures that you've broken the world record for roller coaster rides in a year. You're delighted to be a world record holder and eagerly await the new edition's release, only to find that they've used a fat picture of you next to your entry.

The Zoo

Your Aunt Juanita has always chosen unusual gifts. Recently, she's been on a kick where she gives "charitable" gifts. For example, three Christmases ago, she gave you a card which said that an African child would be immunized against polio from a donation in your name. While that was cool, you really wanted mukluks. For your last birthday, you got a tree. Planted in your name. In Jerusalem. You guess it would be nice if the two sides met in its shade and resolved their difference with smiles and hugs, but you *still* don't have those mukluks. This year, she's really outdone herself. A nice brooch? No. A $2 bill in a Snoopy card? Nope. She's "adopted" you an anteater from the local zoo. You can't take it home, and it's already named Wendell so you don't get to name it, but since Juanita paid for its feed for the year you get to go to the zoo and "meet" it. Was this really easier than a $25 Starbucks gift card?

One Week Later

You're not terribly excited about meeting Wendell, but he's paid for, so you decide to pay him a visit. The keeper shows you into the anteater enclosure and hands you a couple of ounces of loose freeze-dried ants to feed him. You spend a few a few minutes cooing and calling to Wendell to try to get him to come eat the ants, but he stays in the corner and regards you with a cool suspicion. You decide to cut your losses and go look at the other animals.

One Week, One Hour Later

Look at those kangaroos. They don't care what anyone thinks. Hoppin', boppin', chillin' out in the sun. . . . You wonder if the Outback Steakhouse commercials are true, and everything in Australia has this good-natured "fuck work" attitude. One way to find out! You purchase a one-way ticket down under.

One Month Later

Australia's attitude turns out to be less "fuck work" and more "fuck you." Everything is poisonous, including the overhopped local lager. You got sunburned so bad you had to go to the hospital, which in Australia consists of one middle-aged woman in a Red Cross T-shirt saying, "Well, it's sunburn all roight!" You tried to visit an Aboriginal reservation to explore their ancient spirituality, but every time you asked about the Rainbow Serpent they blew a didgeridoo in your face to shut you up. You try to buy a ticket home, but a recent market scare has crippled the value of the U.S. dollar, and you no longer have the money to return.

Six Weeks Later

Forced to work under the table to earn flight money, you start fighting on the underground kangaroo boxing circuit. It's not a proud living, but it's honest.

Hitchhiking

You're on the verge of a tremendous achievement. When you graduated from high school, you made list of things you wanted to accomplish before you were thirty, and at twenty-nine and a half, you've almost done them all. You've been to Europe (granted, it was a four-hour lay-over at Charles de Gaulle, but still). You've climbed a mountain (on a ski lift, but it was still bracing). And most importantly, you've fallen in love (with the bold flavors of Cajun cuisine, which are more constant than any woman). In fact, there's only one experience left on your list: hitchhiking. You don't care where you go or with whom; you just want to gather some tales of the open road. You make a cardboard sign that reads "Next Stop: Adventure!" and pick a spot by the highway. You've got a thumb, a backpack, and six accrued sick days. The world is your oyster.

One Hour Later

You've gotten a ride on a big rig with a trucker named Carl, who's driving a consignment of pantyhose to Idaho Falls. He says the price of a ride is a story, so you start telling him about the time you got fired from your internship at the DNC for stealing toner.

One Hour and Thirty Minutes Later

You barely got to the part where everything everyone printed in the office was very faint and no one could figure out what was going on when Carl stops you and suggests you just play car games.

Two Hours Later

Carl is a beefy man, and after a half-hour of Slug-Bug your whole left side is black and blue. You meekly suggest trying to see who can remember the most state capitals.

Two Hours, Five Minutes Later

"Richmond." "Baton Rouge." "Augusta." "Anchorage." Carl stops you and insists that Juneau is the capital of Alaska, but you stick to your guns. A heated debate ensues, with Carl becoming increasingly irate.

Four Hours Later

Carl blows past the exit for Idaho Falls. You ask if he didn't need to turn off there, but he barks that some things are more important than smooth, sexy legs. At first, you worry that he plans to kill you, but as you near the Canadian border you start to wonder if something even stranger is afoot.

Fifty-One Hours Later

After a tense, nearly wordless two days, Carl pulls into downtown Juneau and makes you get out of the cab in front of the capitol building. He points to the dome and says, "See, wiseass? *Juneau, Alaska.*" "Yeah, well, I let you slide on Baltimore!" you shout. "It's *Annapolis!*" Carl peels out, leaving you stranded.

Fifty-Two Hours Later

You try to take a tour of the building, since you're there, but it's closed for remodeling. You write "Bus Station" on the other side of your sign and trudge toward the highway.

Skiing

You and your girlfriends have gone skiing every winter for years. You're especially excited about going this year, because you managed to land reservations at a resort near Sundance, while the film festival will be going on. You figure you can hit the slopes by day, then if you're feeling adventurous go into town and catch a few movies and indie celebrity sightings. Realistically, you'll spend the evenings in the chalet drinking hot chocolate and playing cribbage, but it's nice to pretend you'll soak up some culture. Skis? Check. Brightly colored, wind-resistant garb? Check. Totally sick powder? *Check.* You are ready to roll.

One Hour Later

You pass a cluster of snowboarders yammering about "catching big air" and "feel just like Shaun White." You have nothing but contempt for them. Snowboarding is to skiing as Dane Cook is to Oscar Wilde.

Three Hours Later

You're gliding down the slope when a tall, lanky figure zips in front of you. You try to swerve and avoid her, but you're not fast enough. You collide and roll down the hill in a disordered clot of limbs, Day-Glo, and curses.

Three Hours, Ten Minutes Later

You disentangle yourself and are startled to see that the woman you hit is the always elegant, rarely pronounceable, never correctly spelled Maggie Gyllenhaal, who had decided to get in a little skiing and "alone time." She's glad you enjoyed *Mona Lisa Smile*, and she'd be happy to talk about her craft under other circumstances, but she thinks she did something pretty bad to her ankle and would like you to flag down ski patrol if you're not busy.

Six Hours Later
You follow La Gyllanhaal to the emergency room, despite her protests and offer to give you $500 to go away and be quiet. Her ankle is badly broken: nothing requiring surgery, but she'll be out of commission for at least six weeks.

One Day Later
La Gyllenhall's injury forces her to drop out of her current project, *Secretary II: Corporate Ties*. You'll be sued for damages by the studio unless you find them a replacement actress.

Two Days Later
Filming resumes on *Secretary II*, with you now in the featured role.

One Year Later
You win a Sundance award for "Special Jury Prize for Spirit of Independence" for your portrayal of a woman bound by her ethics and a series of leather straps.

On the Cast of *The Real World*

Fresh out of a bad relationship and looking to start over, you and a half-metabolized bottle of chardonnay decide to send in an audition tape to be on MTV's *The Real World: Albuquerque*. Despite not being a Wiccan with AIDS or a gay single dad, you're chosen to join the zanily diverse cast. Every season needs The Sheltered White Girl Who Doesn't Realize They're Not "Orientals" Anymore, and your drunken admission that you've never really gotten Martin Luther and Martin Luther King straight in your mind made you a shoo-in. You waxed your upper lip, refilled your Zoloft, and here you are in Albuquerque, eager to meet your seven new best friends.

One Hour Later

Good news: You get the "New Mexico Heroes Room," featuring a mural of Sandra Day O'Connor, Neil Patrick Harris, and Demi Moore on horseback, watching the sun set over the mesa.

Bad news: You have to share it with Oracle, a nineteen-year-old Virgo from Hawaii with Crohn's Disease and a *lot* to talk about.

One Month Later

On camera, you get punched in the face by Joaquin, a dyslexic transman, for referring to HIR transitioning genitals as "The Magical Mystery Tour."

Two Months Later

You're officially pegged as the house "villain" after an ill-advised tribute to Stacey Dash, disastrous both because Stacey Dash is still very much alive (and in a Kanye West video) and because of your unabashed reference to yourself as a "glass of sass."

Two Months and Three Days Later

Unable to stand the hostility, you fake a pregnancy and leave the show midseason. Fuck turquoise jewelry, fuck garlands of dried chili peppers, fuck Albuquerque, and fuck you, *Oracle*.

One Year Later

Missing the limelight and anxious to make rent, you release an album of acoustic Christian rock.

One Year and One Day Later

It receives only one review by the *Sacramento Bee*, titled "Putting the 'God' Back in 'God-Awful.'"

Two Years Later

Broke and with an unflattering new hair color, you agree to go on a *Real World/Road Rules* challenge to recoup the money lost from self-producing your album.

Two Years and Six Months Later

The season ends and you leave the jungles of Brazil slightly less in debt and with a broken arm and bragging rights that you made out on a zipline with celebrity host Mark Hoppus. You may have not won back America's heart, but you *did* score a lifetime backstage pass to the Warped Tour. It's a start.

The Peace Corps

Despite what the Career Day flyers said, it turns out your new degree in International Relations qualifies you to do exactly two things: be U.S. ambassador to Ghana or join the Peace Corps. And since the United States already has an ambassador in Ghana, it looks like you'll be spending the next two years in Eritrea, the Jan Brady to Ethiopia's Marsha, digging irrigation trenches and teaching area children about hand washing. You're ready to roll up your sleeves and show them what a Bennington College girl can do!

Six Months Later

Water moves through your irrigation canals like Miller Lite through a freshman. The local crops produce a good harvest for the first time in 462 years.

Seven Months Later

Now that they have clean hands and are no longer falling over dead from scurvy, malnutrition, and a baker's dozen of wacky tropical fevers, the local villagers finally have the energy to fight against their corrupt central government, and ask you to organize a town meeting. You approach this task with the same energy you spent organizing Bennington's College Democrats.

Eight Months Later

Clashes begin between the loosely organized resistance and government forces—and it's just like the pickup games of Capture the Flag you used to organize at Bennington! The government forces are better opponents than the College Libertarians, but only barely.

Eleven Months Later

Your band of rebels smashes through the government lines, and you capture the capitol at Asmara. You are carried into the Presidential Palace on the shoulders of hundreds of cheering Eritreans. You wish you had worn a bra with better support, but they proclaim you queen anyway.

Two Years Later

You declare war on Yemen, Djibouti, Ethiopia, and the Sudan and proceed to own those bitches.

Forty-Six Years Later

You have ruled Eritrea for a generation. You have brought peace and prosperity to the land, but your habit of casually shooting those foolhardy enough to oppose you is beginning to alienate the country's youth, and there is unrest in the east.

Forty-Six Years and Six Months Later

The rebels have toppled your government, and you've been detained on a decades-old International Court of Justice warrant. You'll be the first Bennington girl to go on trial for war crimes at The Hague!

A War Reenactment

A master's degree in history is like a sixth toe: it's kind of cool to have, but there's not a lot you can do with it. You sent out seventy-eight job applications, and wound up with two options: teaching public high school, or taking on the role of a historical reenactor at PastVille, a premier historical theme park and Pennsylvania's twelfth most visited tourist attraction. Just the thought of all those teenagers is giving you acid reflux, so you're PA bound! You're almost excited about your new job as you arrive on the first day, but that's probably just the gin.

One Hour Later

As "the new kid," you don't get to be in any of the popular wars like Revolutionary, Civil, or WWII. You're given your choice of World War I or the Philippine Rebellion. You choose the former in hopes of getting to wear a spike-topped German helmet.

Two Hours Later

As "the new kid," you have to be the Ottoman army. Not *in* it, you *are* it. You are given a uniform (complete with fez), some training materials about diversity in the workplace, and a wooden musket, and told to be ready for the one o'clock show of the Battle of Gallipoli.

Five Hours Later

Now, you're the first to say you overreacted. But it *is* your first day, you've always been a little high-strung, and you panicked. The sight of the "entire Australia–New Zealand Army Corps," which is only five guys but five BIG guys, scared the piss out of you. You knew it was all a show, but did they? *Why are their bayonets so shiny?* Before you knew it, you had dropped your gun, wet yourself, and run screaming into the woods surrounding the park. The audience loved it: everyone loves a good pee-in-the-pants gag.

Nine Hours Later

How are you this lost? You can't have been running into the woods for more than ten minutes, but you can't find your way back to the park. Your blood sugar is a little low . . . surely any berries growing in Pennsylvania can't be that poisonous. You'll limit yourself to a small handful to be safe.

Nine Hours, Fifteen Minutes Later

You can taste time, and you are suddenly sure that *they* are following you.

One Day Later

Terrorist Plot Foiled By Campers (Ap)

State College, PA—Joe Bradley and his son Todd got more than they bargained for on their annual camping trip in the Appalachian Mountains. The two men were fishing when a disheveled man in a urine-stained Turkish army uniform accosted them and began screaming about "getting back to camp" and "showing those damn Australians." The Bradleys overpowered the man and turned him over to local law enforcement, where he is being held pending transfer to the detention facility at Guantanamo Bay.

A Wedding (Uninvited)

You don't say it enough—you *couldn't* say it enough—but God bless Vince Vaughn. You had always attributed your limited success with women to your "more taquitos, please" body type and the "another vodka tonic, please" puffiness around your eyes, but then you saw *Wedding Crashers*. Here's this guy who looks like the poor man's Kevin James, and he's up to his *ears* in broads, just by being loud, drunk, abrasive, and present! It turns out the ruby slippers were on your feet all along, but instead of clicking your heels three times you just annoy celebrating women until one of them beds you to shut you up. *You had the power all along.* You look through the social events page of the paper, and note that a big wedding is planned for tomorrow afternoon. You will be there.

You Arrive

You still can't tell if your slacks are black or navy, but you've put on a full ounce of Old Spice and trimmed your pubic hair, so you're as ready as you can be. You're a tad overexcited, so you arrive at the venue a full hour before the wedding is planned to start. Luckily, a lot of other people are there, chatting and mingling, so you take the plunge.

Thirty Minutes Later

Oh my *God.* You've spent the last fifteen minutes chatting with a girl. She is Asian, her name is Crystal, and she's on her fourth Singapore Sling—according to *Maxim*, any one of those traits means she's a sure thing, so all three . . . yowza. She touches your leg and says she needs to go fill out some paperwork, but would you like to join her for the ceremony, and afterwards. You respond with what you hope is a not-too-desperately-grateful yes, and she asks for your driver's license.

Odd, but you convince yourself she wants to show you off to her girl-friends in the ladies' room.

One Hour Later

Everyone has formed up in an orderly pattern on the lawn. You can't see the bride and groom from where you are, nor can you hear what the minister is saying. Crystal seems excited, though, and keeps smiling at you and squeezing your hand (oh yes, ladies and gentlemen, you're *holding her hand*). You notice that everyone in the crowd seems to be paired off, and as you begin to comment on that to Crystal, the minister begins to applaud, and Crystal grabs your head and kisses you. It's the coolest thing ever until she pulls back slightly and murmurs, "My husband." Looking around, you notice that everyone is kissing and exchanging rings. You just pulled off the most dubious coup in uninvited guest history: you crashed a mass wedding and became one of the grooms. It no longer matters that you didn't catch Crystal's last name, because she has yours now. Also half of everything you own.

Four Months Later

You were willing to give it a shot—you know, kismet, we'll tell our grandkids, etc.—but Crystal took one look at the temperate forest's-worth of Wendy's bags on your apartment floor and filed divorce papers. You tried to get back in the groove by crashing another wedding—Jewish this time—but your attempt to "blend in" by stomping on a champagne glass failed when a shard cut through your boat shoe and you had to go to the emergency room. MongolianBridez.biz is sounding less and less like a last resort.

LARP

As secrets go, yours isn't a particularly shocking one. No illegitimate births, no cases of Kentucky Deluxe "the budget whiskey" in the closet, no missing cheerleaders buried in the crawlspace. You've merely always wanted to give LARPing a shot. LARP stands for "live action role play," and is a game—some would say lifestyle—in which people take on fantasy personas and act out a story. Imagine an outdoor, moving-around, less-Mountain-Dew "Dungeons and Dragons." You don't know why, but you've always wanted to pop on a leather jerkin and fight the duke's men in an intense Nerf battle. Cool is for losers; LARPing sounds *fun*. Nevertheless, you are a little worried. Against all odds, you've recently landed a sweet finance job at Barclay, Barclay, Worthington, and Barclay, Delaware's sixth most prestigious investment firm. You imagine Messrs. Barclay et al. would look down on your medieval woodland exploits, but you've decided to live a little and give LARPing a shot. What could go wrong?

One Hour Later

You arrive at the park, sign in at a card table manned by a "gobliness" in a leather bustier, and join up with your team. The object of today's game is to find three sacred treasures with which to vanquish a demon that beleaguers the kingdom: the Mirror of Courage, the Emerald of Tolerance, and the Sword of Meaningful Health Care Reform. There's an odd "Nancy Pelosi's Birthday Scavenger Hunt" vibe, but you decide to stay because a wench in a low-cut blouse is offering you a horn of mead.

Three Hours Later

Liberal subtext or not, this quest is awesome. You're drunk on mead, scampering around the woods with cleavage-packing maidens, and you've found the Emerald of Tolerance in a magical tree.

Three and a Half Hours Later

Yet drunker on mead and wench cleavage, and bearing the newly-discovered Sword of Meaningful Health Care Reform aloft, you stumble across a picnicking family. As you open your mouth to bellow something about infidels and the King's Peace, you notice that the father of this picnicking family is Barry from Sales, one of your coworkers . . . and an asshole. Maybe, just maybe, he didn't recognize you?

Two Days Later

Nope, he definitely did recognize you, judging by this excerpt from his sales report at the weekly meeting: "We must continue on our quest to vanquish the competition, yea, as though they were ogres, and to rescue the damsel of profits and the jewels of increased market share from the dragon that is market volatility."

Seven Days Later

You quit your job after the forty-third time someone refers to you as "Prince Valiant."

Seven Weeks Later

To make ends meet, you take a job flipping burgers, and what do you know? It turns out that your new manager is Gary from the LARP group, and he's thrilled at the chance to incorporate the game into his job. Most recently, you have been instructed to prepare every Whopper as though it were for the table of the king himself.

The Eiffel Tower

Ah, Paris. It wasn't cheap, but you sold a barrel of plasma and used a twelve-year-old student ID, and bought a cheap ticket to France. You'd always dreamed of going, and now you're there. It's everything you'd hoped it would be: the seductive odor of the spring flowers, the wine and women in Montmartre, the incomparable *Frenchness* of a stroll down the Champs-Élysées. After a light breakfast of fruit and croissants, you walk out of your hotel smiling and eager because this is *the* day. This is the day you go see the Eiffel Tower—jewel of France, triumph of architecture, and your favorite phallic symbol, hands down. One last glance at the map, one last adjustment of your beret, and you're on your way.

Fifteen Minutes Later

Thirteen euros to take an elevator up a glorified cell phone tower? Fine, you'll pay, but the next time the Germans get all up in their grill these chintzy Frogs can just ask some *other* superpower for help.

Thirty Minutes Later

You're at the top of the tower and overwhelmed by your emotions, principally "Oh God, it's so high up," "one gust of wind and this baby goes down like a pile of toothpicks," and "shitshitshitshit."

Seven Hours Later

The guards are trying to close the tower for the night, but you refuse to leave the one spot on the viewing platform you consider architecturally sound. There's no way you're walking around on this deathtrap and then taking an *elevator* through the pile of unstable rebar these people call a monument. The guards argue that the tower has stood since 1889 and survived both world wars. This does not convince you.

Eight Hours Later

The police have been called, and one shoots you with a dart hoping they can get you into the elevator unconscious. The tranquilizer only makes you irritable and sleepy.

Seventeen Hours Later

Apparently, this same thing happened to a Japanese lady in the 1980s and they got her off with a helicopter. This option is not open to you, though; the new French austerity budget replaced the helicopter squad with one guy in a hang glider and he's busy sightseeing over Provence.

Fifty-Six Years Later

Famed Eccentric Dies in France (Where Else?)

PARIS (AP) Paris wears black today. One of the city's most beloved eccentrics, the Tower Man [this is you, by the by], has died. American by birth, the Tower Man made headlines in late 2012 when he climbed to the top of the Eiffel Tower and refused to leave, citing safety concerns and a case of the Mondays. He quickly became an added draw to the already magnetic landmark, and tourists and Parisians alike enjoyed feeding him scraps and adding sticks to the makeshift shelter he constructed on the observation deck. An anonymous donor has paid for him to be buried in the famed Père Lachaise Cemetery.

And the best part is, you got an even better spot than Jim Morrison!

On *The Price Is Right*

You have loved *The Price is Right* longer and harder than anything else in the world, including parents, girlfriends, and beer. Your earliest childhood memory is of a heavyset woman kissing Bob Barker on the lips after winning a breakfront by correctly guessing the price of a canister of "Jane's Krazy Mixed-Up Salt," and as a schoolchild you used to leave a slice of baloney on the radiator overnight and then eat it so you could throw up, stay home from school, and watch Bob's Beauties lovingly caress the sponsors' products—oh, to be that bottle of Pine-Sol! Finally, after years of watching and constructing a rickety home Plinko board in your garage, your friends chipped in and bought you a round-trip ticket to "historic Studio 33 at CBS Television City in Hollywood, California." You've been in line by the studio door since 3 A.M., wearing your handmade puff-paint "I BRAKE FOR BEAUTIES" T-shirt and wielding your "I Heart Drew Carey" foam finger. Despite this wardrobe choice, they let you in anyway, and you're ready to roll.

Five Minutes Later

"Edmund Harrington, come on down! You're the next contestant on *The Price Is Right!*" God is real, and he's not mad about all the *Playboys* under your mattress.

Ten Minutes Later

What does everyone else think is so special about that knife set? It's Japanese. *Everyone* knows the true capital of knife artistry is South Korea. You successfully undercut everyone by bidding $1 and are called onto the stage.

Eleven Minutes Later

It's Plinko. Your friends laughed when you built a practice Plinko board, but you wonder if they're laughing now as you rattle off accurate prices for the sample items, then expertly guide all five discs into the $10,000 slot. Plink, plink, plink, plink, plink, ka-ching.

Twenty-Eight Minutes Later

You're ready to spin the big wheel for your chance to enter the Show-case Showdown. You grab the handle, jump up in the air, and pull on the wheel with all your might. You realize something is wrong even as you let go; a few snaps are heard, then a crunch, and the giant wheel has torn itself loose from its moorings. Before anyone can react, the wheel barrels toward host Drew Carey, America's sweetheart and a healthy-size inspiration to billions, and badly injures him.

Four Hours Later

You're in trouble for accidentally maiming a national icon—apparently this not only is sad but also violates several union rules—but they're letting you keep the knife set!

A Cross-Country Road Trip

Britney Spears has romanticized a lot of things—pop stardom, Louisiana, living like a high-class toilet seat—but she may have been on to something with her 2002 rom-com, *Crossroads*. The film is hilarious (though mostly unintentionally), but more important, it makes taking a cross-country road trip seem like a genuinely good idea. Feeling inspired, you and your best friend have decided to cash in your 401(k)s, rent a car, and drive through all forty-eight contiguous states, making a pit stop in each to visit a wacky tourist trap. Clear the road—you've got places to see and souvenir shot glasses to buy.

Five Days Later

You learn that, as it turns out, lucrative highway karaoke competitions aren't as commonplace as the movie *Crossroads* would have you believe. (Unless that was just an early '00s kind of thing. Like Napster or Razor scooters.)

One Week Later

In West Virginia you learn that truck drivers don't like it when you replace Def Leppard on the jukebox with Britney Spears, and despite what your best friend's Christmas card said last year, she will *not* always have your back.

One Week and Four Days Later

In Nebraska, you decide to stop in Boys Town—a community-driven organization dedicated to rehabilitating at-risk youth, *not* the gayest stretch of five blocks in America, as you might guess from the name—to see the world's largest stamp ball.

One Week, Four Days, and Two Hours Later

Once inside Boys Town's Stamp Center, you don't realize that the tour guide is calling you "son" less as a term of endearment and more because she's misinterpreted your baby face, graduated bob, and admittedly "tomboy" cargo shorts as proof positive that you're one of their wayward boys starting anew.

One Week, Four Days, and Three Hours Later

As the tour ends, you thank your guide, reach into (one of your many) pockets, pull out your car keys, and walk toward the door. Suddenly, a hand lands on your shoulder, twirls you around, and the guide motions toward your keys and asks where you think you're going. You try to explain to her that you're just in town to see the ball of stamps and need to get back on the road, but the guide has already called a code red on her walky-talky and two public safety Crown Victorias have pulled up in front of the building.

One Week, Four Days, and Eight Hours Later

No amount of Massachusetts state ID flashing, best friend vouching, parent calling, or pant dropping can convince these people that you're a mild-mannered lesbian from Groton, *not* a troubled youth seeking asylum, and you end up having to go to reform school for a couple of years.

One Year Later

It's inconvenient at first, but it really helps you turn your life around.

A Murder Mystery Dinner Party

Dinner at the Rosenthals' tends to be a bit of a snoozer. The brisket is always overcooked, Stan and Harriet spend the entire night bickering about whether they're strict enough with their son Herschel, and Morty always makes the same joke where he pretends to serve the Manischewitz before he brings out the real wine. You thought about declining their most recent invitation and pleading trouble with the ol' tonsils, but then you found out that this month's dinner party was to be one of those themed murder mystery dinners and the pain cleared right up. You love murder mystery novels and read so many that your wife has started to make passive-aggressive comments about your "torrid affair" with Sue Grafton. Now you're at the party looking for clues and you're ready to show your wife that B is for Bitch.

One Hour Later

It's only been an hour and you've cracked the case like the tail of this flavorless lobster. "Only the colonel, from his years in India, would have known of the poisonous properties of the exotic oleander shrub. It could have only have been he who introduced the lethal blossoms into the Duchess's evening toddy." At this point your wife tells you to sit down and stop embarrassing her.

One Week Later

Drunk on your success at the Rosenthals', you begin sleuthing around the house. "The Case of the Missing Car Keys." "The Case of the Your Curfew Is at Eleven, and Not a Minute After, Young Man." It's starting to annoy your family, but they're just going to have to accept that this is your vocation. Would you tell a bird not to sing?

Two Weeks Later

You've started wearing a deerstalker cap and smoking a pipe. The pipe makes you nauseous, but we all have to suffer for our art.

Three Weeks Later

Your sleuthing continues unabated: you just found the cat. Also you were so caught up in detecting that you burst into your son's room unannounced and accidentally solved "The Mystery of Where Did the Hand Lotion Go?"

One Month Later

During some routine detective work, you find a pile of motel rental receipts and inadvertently find out that your wife is cheating on you. You decide some things are better left undiscovered, hang up your deerstalker cap, and curl up with a good Sue Grafton novel—but not before pouring sugar in your wife's gas tank, that is. E is for Engine Trouble!

Your High School Reunion

It's hard to believe it's been ten years since high school. Not much has changed: you still live at home, you still have a part-time job at Fry's Electronics, and you still buy your weed from Derrick, the middle school's janitor. When your mom handed you the invitation to your ten-year high school reunion (and reminded you to get all the Mountain Dew bottles out of your bedroom before they get moldy), you were torn. Do you skip it to drink a six-pack of Molson Ice in your parent's basement with the guys like you did on prom night, or do you go and hope your long-time crush, Brittany Atkinson, is both present and profoundly desperate? It's a stumper. In the end, you decide to avoid having the "Why don't you go? You should go," conversation with your mom by simply going.

Ten Minutes Later

Brittany Atkinson is there. With her husband, child, and peg leg. Three strikes and one glance has to be some kind of record.

Twenty Minutes Later

Oh, Doug Miller is a state senator. You're not even sure if you've ever voted.

Thirty Minutes Later

You ask Laura Hernandez to dance and she calmly blows her rape whistle. A simple no would have sufficed.

Forty Minutes Later

As the homecoming court takes the stage to tell the story of how they all got their real estate licenses, you sidle up to the bar and say, "Amaretto Sours—line 'em up."

One Hour Later

After a cool dozen Amaretto Sours and a shot of Jägermeister, you quietly vomit into a potted palm and make your way home.

One Hour and Thirty Minutes Later

Once home, suffering a crippling attack of the drunk munchies, you decide to reheat the remnants of last night's burrito. Just as you start the microwave, you realize you forgot to take the tin foil off and sparks begin to fly. A ray of pure light shoots through the microwave glass and hits you in the chest. It's not pleasant, but it doesn't seem to kill you, and by the time you check yourself for injuries, the burrito is done. You find that as soon as you think about opening the microwave oven and extracting your dinner, the door opens and the burrito floats out and lands in your hand.

Two Hours Later

After eating your burrito (no sense letting it get cold), you practice with your newfound powers. You find that you can easily pick up the DVD case, remove the *Family Guy* disc, and start the episode where Peter Griffin confronts his own mortality without ever having to lift a finger.

Two Hours and Ten Minutes Later

You consider using your powers for good but then your mom would find out that you microwaved metal and there would be a disagreement. Best let sleeping dogs lie.

The Local Library

As far as Kansas City summers go, this one is particularly awful. It's a *scorcher*. Your house doesn't have central air, and you've grown tired of lying nude in a kiddie pool filled with ice water in the middle of your living room. (It cools your torso down, but your extremities stay hot.) You thought about going to the mall to cool off, but the manager at Lids asked you not to come back after you pitched a fit over the Knicks hats not accommodating a "full-figured" head. You could always spend the day in the movie theater, but it seems like Katherine Heigl is in everything. You considered cooling off at the municipal pool, but you don't think you'll ever be hot enough to willingly dive into a big bowl of human soup with a chlorine floater. You've decided to go to your local library, which in addition to being free and air-conditioned, is also the gateway to the magical world of reading. Buckle up!

One Hour Later

You open *Are You There God? It's Me, Margaret,* and it hits too close to home. Which is weird considering you're a sixty-four-year-old black man, but then again, I guess nobody ever really feels comfortable in their body. You decide to just use the free Internet for a while.

One Hour and Thirty Minutes Later

You've never been a good speller. Instead of going to FARK.com, the underground news source, you went to FARC.com, the official website for the Revolutionary Armed Forces of Columbia, a left-wing terrorist group. Unbeknownst to you, you land on a government watch list.

One Week Later

You earn your second strike buying raw milk.

One Year Later

You vote for Ralph Nader as a write-in for state comptroller. The government takes notice, and a few days later you receive a form letter explaining that you've been placed on the No Fly List.

Two Years Later

Because of this No Fly List nonsense, you have to take a Greyhound bus to Toronto for your goddaughter's wedding. Only the wheels differentiate the bus from a state mental health facility.

Two Years and One Week Later

You e-mail Cat Stevens to see how he's handling the no-fly situation. He sends you back a signed copy of the *Harold and Maude* soundtrack, a few pamphlets on Islam, and a note that says, "Stay Loose. Love, Yusuf. P.S. Have you heard about Megabus?" You have—they're always late and their Wi-Fi is spotty.

Your Kid's Prom

Sunrise, sunset. It's hard to believe little Bethany is already old enough to go to her senior prom. It feels like just yesterday you were checking the ingredients on her juice box for known allergens and here she is with a driver's license and an acceptance letter to CU-Boulder and everything. A few weeks earlier, she laughingly mentioned that the school was looking for concerned parents to chaperone, "I mean, how lame is that?" Pretty lame, but it also gives you a valuable opportunity to prevent your daughter from losing her virginity on a towel hastily thrown over the seat of a rented stretch Escalade. A mother does what she can.

Two Weeks Later

As a mother, you're glad the punch isn't spiked. As someone who has to listen to a Nickelback medley for about four hours, you'd kill for a pint of Everclear.

Two Weeks and One Hour Later

During your routine "bathroom check" you confiscate a joint and slip out back to "throw it away." As you prepare to burn the joint "so no one can find it and smoke it," you hear muffled sounds from a nearby dumpster. You lift up the lid and are shocked to see a real live, honest-to-goodness prom night dumpster baby in among the math tests and pizza crusts. You wonder if this is your lucky night.

Two Weeks and Four Hours Later

You bring the baby home, both because you don't want it to end up in the foster care system and because Bethany is going to CU-Boulder in the fall and you don't want to be lonely. You name him Purgamentum, the Latin name for trash—Purgie for short.

Seven Years Later
How can *every* pet on the block go missing in the same week?

Fourteen Years Later
Purgie leaves bloody footprints wherever he goes. You know boys are different than girls, but surely this isn't normal puberty.

Sixteen Years Later
When especially enraged, Purgie's eyes go bloodshot and his head spins all the way around. You *knew* you shouldn't have let him play football, but it seemed like such a healthy outlet for a growing young boy.

Thirty Years Later
In fulfillment of Biblical prophecy, Purgie (or Purgamentum as he now insists on being called) has united the world's governments, destroyed Jerusalem, and decreed that everyone must be tattooed with the number 666. It's become painfully apparent that the dumpster baby you rescued years ago has grown up to be the Antichrist. But at least you raised him to have good table manners!

A First-Class Seat

Of all the little luxuries you grant yourself (weekly mani/pedi, Whitman's samplers, a mojito when out with the girls), flying first-class is not one of them. You'd like to, but it's just not realistic on the salary of an HR manager of a struggling Hertz Rent-A-Car franchise. However, you've decided to treat yourself this time: If they're going to send you all the way to Spokane to attend a conference, you feel you deserve some leg room and domestic sparkling wine along the way. You've got your travel capris on and a Xanax in your purse. As a first-class passenger, you get to board first, so you take a seat next to a lady in a fur coat, kick back, and watch the common folk straggle in. The waiter comes by with a menu and sachet of Jordan almonds and you think you could get used to this.

One Hour Later

You're still sitting on the tarmac waiting for a low-pressure area over Idaho to dissipate. Normally you'd be furious at the delay, but they're placating the first-class passengers with caviar and champagne. You suppose you can be patient until Sven works his way over to you.

Three Hours Later

You still haven't moved, there's unrest in the cheap seats, but at least you have this complimentary turducken to occupy your time!

Five Hours Later

You're still stuck. Thankfully you can entertain yourself by watching streaming Netflix on the complimentary HD plasma screen built into the seat in front of you. Back in coach their entertainment choices are limited to sitting quietly or watching a Ken Burns documentary.

Six Hours Later

The peasants have been pushed to the breaking point. From behind the privacy curtain you hear someone shout, "Forward, comrades!" and a flood of budget travelers overpowers the stewardess and surges into the first-class cabin, murder in their eyes. You begin to protest that no— you're poor! You're just like them! You steal toilet paper from Burger King! But it falls on deaf ears. They tear you and your fellow first-class passengers limb from limb, force open the airplane door, and march up and down the tarmac using your abused bodies as props in their rallying cry.

One Day Later

The airline offers the revolutionaries each a $200 flight voucher and tweets an apology.

Vacation

After six weeks of corpse like immobility, you're finally nearly over this bout of mono. (You should have never agreed to volunteer in that kissing booth, but it was just such a good cause.) Now that you can finally stand without fainting and swallow without crying, you've decided to treat yourself to a recuperation week at Sandals, Montego Bay, in sunny, homophobic Jamaica. It'll do you some good to get out of the house and out of that same ratty terry cloth robe. If rum, sun, and a little "just friends" romp with a busboy named Winston doesn't cure your ills, nothing will.

One Week Later
Turns out the busboy's name is Neville, but other than that, the fantasy is pretty much just as you imagined.

One Week, Two Days Later
Tired of sticking close to the resort playing Strip Bridge with Neville, you rent a scooter and hit the road to discover the "real" Jamaica.

One Week, Three Days Later
You're in a jerk chicken hut surrounded by "real" Jamaicans, each of whom has a joint. They think it's cute that you wandered away from the resort and have decided to smoke you up while explaining basic tenets of Rastafarianism. It makes a lot of sense to you.

Two Weeks Later
While your relationship with Neville may have been a flash in the pan, your new connection to Rastafarianism is not. Now back home in Fairfield, Connecticut, you've purchased a Vespa and painted it the

red, yellow, and green of African unity. You ride it proudly to your job at Starbucks, where you get in trouble for your new "Africans Unite!" tattoo. They're *really* not going to be happy when you have your long blonde hair dreaded.

Two Weeks, Two Days Later

You take down your Tegan and Sara poster and replace it with a self-made Photoshop print of Bob Marley, Haile Selassie, and the Lion of Judah sharing a spliff and looking upward toward a glorious future.

Three Weeks Later

Your mother refuses to have another conversation with you until you stop saying "Babylon," "Excuse I," and "mon."

One Month Later

While jumping up and down on your bed and rocking out to the soundtrack of *Cool Runnings*, one of your dreadlocks gets hooked over a blade of the ceiling fan. The sudden jerk breaks your neck and you meet your Rasta Maker.

Eternity

It turns out you were a pretty good Rastafarian, no matter how silly you looked, so your soul goes to life everliving in Ethiopia and you and Jah spend eternity listening to dance hall music and making fun of the losers in Presbyterian heaven.

Antiquing

You and your husband have planned a romantic weekend driving through New England to watch the foliage turn. You decide to do it right and do a little antiquing while you're already up there in America's attic. As you drive along the Merritt Parkway, you see a sign for an antique store's closeout and stop to investigate. The man running the sale explains that the "merry old homosexual" who owned this antique store has recently passed away, and his company has been hired to liquidate the inventory. You spot an adorable little hutch and buy it on impulse. It's going to be a *bear* to get in your Volvo S80, but it's worth it—it has inlaid handles!

One Week Later

Once home, you think about where to put the hutch and finally put it in the garage until you figure it out.

One Week and One Day Later

You awake the next morning to find that the hutch has mysteriously relocated to the dining room. You don't know why it's there, but the more you think about it, it will be an excellent conversation piece.

One Week and Two Days Later

You come home from work and discover that your living room has been completely rearranged. You find this peculiar because your husband is away on business, but also note that the general "flow" of the room is much improved.

One Week and Three Days Later

"Where the hell did that fern come from, and why does it bring the whole room together?"

One Week and Four Days Later

The mysterious new Thomas Kincaid print in the kitchen really makes you not mind spending time in there!

One Week and Five Days Later

One day, you find the following message written in blood on your wall: "Dear Pam: I thought it would only be polite to drop you a line and explain myself. My name is Chester Quinn and my partner Terry and I used to own the antique store you stopped in a few weeks ago. When I died, my soul became trapped in the hutch that I was polishing at the time, which you and your husband later bought. I didn't want to seem presumptuous, but I thought your décor needed a few little touches to make the most of the space. Also, not to be a bitchy old queen, but have you thought about having some lowlights in your hair? I really think it would take out some of the roundness in your face. Best, Chester." The message is in a tasteful, elegant font and well centered on the wall, so you leave it up as an accent piece.

Twenty Years Later

Now a treasured member of the family, Chester goes with your daughter to Swarthmore to help her set up her dorm room.

Your College Homecoming

When you were in college, you hated it. Now that you've graduated and are living in the real world, however, you would do anything to go back. Oh, how you long for the days of raucous frat parties, afternoon catnaps, and girls who would do practically anything because hey, they were in college. Society keeps telling you that those days are over and it's not "acceptable" to wear bike shorts with a can of Milwaukee's Best tucked in the waistband anymore, but for one glorious weekend, you get to go back and relive the dream. It's called Homecoming and it's calling your name. You load up the car, paint "BISON OR BUST!" on the rear windshield, pick up your old college buddies, and peel out.

One Day Later

You're back on campus. First stop: the dining hall. Gotta carbo load for the long weekend ahead.

One Day and One Hour Later

You try to go up to your old dorm room to haze the freshman currently living there, but security won't let you. You try flashing them your Sam's Club card to see if they mistake it for a student ID and it only complicates things further.

One Day and Two Hours Later

You successfully complete a "Power Hour" by drinking an ounce of beer a minute for a full hour.

One Day and Three Hours Later

You go to the school store and stock up on pennants. Better to have them and not need them than to need them and not have them.

One Day and Four Hours Later

You sit in on an enormous freshman seminar in Foundations of Western Civilizations expecting to scam on some girls. Instead, you learn a great deal about the birth of monotheism and resolve to learn more at your local library.

One Day and Seven Hours Later

After doing a few keg stands at your old fraternity house, you and your buddies start feeling a little rambunctious. You decide to sneak over to the house of your sister sorority and launch a good old-fashioned no-holds-barred panty raid. The fraternity brothers still in college stop you and tell you that the Tri Delts had to move off campus six months ago after a hazing violation in which they forced a diabetic girl to eat a fistful of Domino sugar, and the building was taken over by the Campus Feminist Alliance. You'd like to be able to cancel the panty raid, you really would, but once a panty raid has been declared, you cannot stop it for any reason. Check your bylaws, brah.

One Day, Seven Hours, and Thirty Minutes Later

It turns out that they don't have drawers full of panties at the ready in the Campus Feminist Alliance, but they do have a burglar alarm. You get busted by campus security and have to spend the rest of the weekend picking up litter on the quad.

An Open Mic Night

Ever since your mother started "The Change," she's really gotten in touch with the woman inside. She's stopped dyeing her hair, started wearing flowy dresses, and has bought a quarry's worth of raw stone jewelry. You're trying to be supportive, so you've agreed to accompany her to an open mic night where she will sing Celtic songs and accompany herself on the acoustic guitar. On the night of her gig, you escort her into a dimly lit coffee shop where a plump man in heavy mascara is on-stage singing a sexually explicit version of "Kumbaya." Everyone in the crowd looks like they were a "theater person" in high school and owns at least one "Love Me, Love My Cat" pillow, but your mom looks excited so you're willing to play along.

Fifteen Minutes Later

Your mom goes on-stage and delivers a surprisingly moving rendition of "Whiskey in the Jar" and damn near brings you to tears.

Eighteen Minutes Later

As the applause for your mother dies down, she grabs the mic and announces, "Thank you! I couldn't have done any of this without the support of my son. Sweetheart, come up here!" You bashfully slink on-stage and are horrified when your mother presses the microphone into your hand and tells you to "express yourself" because it's so "freeing."

Twenty Minutes Later

You've been standing on the stage like a deer in headlights for the past two minutes trying to figure out what to do. The audience begins to chant, "EXPRESS! EXPRESS! EXPRESS!" and you buckle under the pressure and perform a slam poetry style repartition of the lyrics to rap artist Mos Def's song "Travelin' Man." The crowd, having never heard of Mos Def, thinks you're a natural poet and goes wild.

One Month Later

Encouraged by your initial impression, you've been going back weekly, each time performing a new Mos Def song as if it were your own slam poetry. You've become the darling of the Asheville beatnik poetry scene and are even featured in the local weekly, which prints a few of your "poems" under the title "The Sultan of Slam."

Three Months Later

Unbeknownst to you, Mos Def has a cousin in Asheville who informs Mr. Def of your plagiarism.

Three Months and One Day Later

One night while you're on-stage smoking a cigarette and reciting the lyrics to "Ms. Fat Booty," Mos Def bursts through the door. You think he has his "posse" with him, but it turns out just to be his crew of entertainment lawyers. He accuses you of "biting his rhymes" and challenges you to a rap battle. After rap-talking the lyrics to the *Three's Company* theme song during your turn, you lose harder than anyone has lost anything in the history of the world. Ever.

Four Months Later

Ruined in Asheville, you move to Richmond and start the process all over again using the work of Tupac Shakur, who is good and dead. (R.I.P.)

CHAPTER 3

Social Graceless

When Relationships Go to Relationshit

At last count, there are seven billion people in the world, uneasily grouped into two hundred countries, sixty-three hundred languages, a baker's dozen's worth of feuding religions, and an ever-expanding roster of genders. In all this confusion, someone will inevitably misinterpret your businesslike eye contact as an aggressive staredown, and before you know it you're bare-knuckle boxing in an alley in Little Osaka. At first glance, it would seem easier and safer to stick with your own kind, but even people you think you understand will sometimes flummox you, flying into rages not over *what* you said but *how* you said it, and refusing to tell you why they're mad because "that's the whole point." You may have the best intentions in the world, but they won't help you when communications break down. The only things that work then are gin and apologies.

Play a Board Game with Friends

It's a rainy night, so you and your friends decide to have Bro Thursday at your house instead of at the traditional End Zonez Bar 'n' Grille. There's nothing good on TV, so you decide to do the next best thing and play a board game. Clue? "No, Randy will just always say 'Randy, with mah dick, in the *bed*room!' for every round." Boggle? "The cube got depressurized when Todd sat on it and now it doesn't work." Yahtzee? "Too much like craps without being enough like craps." All that's left in the closet is Risk, Hasbro's classic game of world domination. It's no football and hot wings, but at least you get to yell and compete.

Five Minutes Later

"Dennis, don't be a prick. You lost the coin toss. You have to be the yellow armies."

Twenty Minutes Later

You've divided the world into your various personal spheres of interest. You've got a strong position in Scandinavia and Ukraine, but you're annoyed that the strategically powerful Australia/New Guinea areas belong to Jeremy, who's just going to spend all night in the bathroom texting his ex-girlfriend about how he's over her pettiness.

Two Hours Later

You all swore you wouldn't get too competitive to avoid a repeat of the infamous time you played a game of Risk for three days straight and got so into it Randy wouldn't get up to go to the bathroom and ultimately had to be catheterized. Just a friendly game among bros.

Five Hours Later

That jackass Todd thinks he can just invade Alberta without conse-quences? We'll let the dice do the talking....

Three Days Later

You've taken several days off work, using as your excuse that you have to take an emergency trip to Venezuela. This is, in the loosest pos-sible sense of the word, true.

Six Days Later

Your wife comes down the stairs laden with suit-cases and informs you that she's moving all her armies to the Motel 6 across town until you decide to act like an adult.

Nine Days Later

If you just break through Irkutsk and take Kamchatka, Asia will be yours. The people will bow to you. Oh, how they'll bow. You take a deep breath as you plan your strategy and notice that you have smelled better.

Eleven Days Later

You win, if losing your wife, job, and reputation for hygiene in order to have the privilege of moving a plastic cannon onto a map of Madagas-car can be considered "winning" in any true sense of the word.

Give Your Kid a Unique Name

You will never forgive your parents for naming you "Anne." It's such a "plain Jane" name, if you will. Your friends all had beautiful, unusual names like Concetta, Melania, and Columbia-Gem-of-the-Ocean, but you were just Anne. Anne the man. Anne the man with the plan. Anne who desperately needs a tan. Anne who eats fruit from a can. No one wants to go to the prom with Anne. Girls named "Tiffany" and "Crystal" are fun to dance with. Girls named "Anne" make sure you get home safe. Girls named "Anne" don't get to go to Vassar with the Charlottes and the Penelopes; they go to Penn State with Sarahs and Kristens. Anne doesn't get to marry Trevor van de Water, captain of the lacrosse team and heir to the van de Water shipping fortune; she has to marry Lester Peabody, who will probably be a good provider despite his fallen arches. You don't want the daughter you're expecting to soldier away under a mediocre name like you had to. You're going to name her something with spice, fire, and promise.

Three Days Later

At 6:24 A.M. you welcome to the world Xaviera Sagittaria Cornucopia Kleopatra Jingleheimer-Schmidt, Xavi-Sagi for short.

Eight Years Later

Xavi-Sagi comes home in tears because a boy at school told her that her name sounded like a brand of inexpensive vaginal cream.

Twelve Years Later

You have to go down to the school to explain to the teacher that no, she's not dyslexic, that's actually how her name is spelled.

Seventeen Years Later

Xavi-Sagi's SAT scores are invalidated because the scorers see her name and assume they're on a poorly conceived prank TV show, à la *Candid Camera*.

Eighteen Years Later

The dispute with the SAT people is dragging on, and a depressed Xavi-Sagi, unable to go to college and embittered by years of taunts and always having to spell her name over the phone, has fallen in with a bad crowd. Her new friends are all sickly looking and wear a lot of pleather. Recently, Xavi-Sagi has started ending her phone calls abruptly when you enter the room, and leaves for days with no explanation.

Eighteen Years, Six Months Later

Xavi-Sagi pulls a Menendez brothers' scheme, conspiring with her friends to kill you for the insurance money and as revenge for ruining her life by giving her such an absurd name. She tried to cut your brake lines, but ultimately only succeeded in ruining your XM radio. At her trial, the judge gives her a suspended sentence, but orders you to perform 200 hours of community service for being an idiot.

Try a Long-Distance Relationship

You thought your heart would break when Fjalar, your Icelandic boyfriend, told you his student visa was expiring and he had to go home to Reykjavik. You swore you'd keep in touch and make the long-distance thing work, and as he held you, there in the red loading zone outside the international terminal of Houston's George Bush airport, you believed it could happen. After all, it's not terribly hard to keep in touch with someone in this day and age, what with computers and such. You swear to join him in Iceland as soon as you can save enough money, and until then you'll call and e-mail faithfully. You don't want to lose this Viking who plundered your heart.

One Week Later

You went to Radio Shack and bought an expensive headphone set with a built-in microphone so you could more easily Skype with Fjalar. You catch him online, but he seems oddly distant. Must be the jet lag.

Two Weeks Later

Fjalar breaks up with you over Skype. It seems he's met a nice Icelandic girl—Bryndís—at a hot spring and plans to marry her and take over the family fishing sloop. He tells you that cod is in his blood, and it never would have worked between you. You're devastated and spend the whole night crying, fantasizing about poisoning the major North Atlantic fisheries, and cutting up the fisherman's sweaters you'd placed in your hope chest.

Four Weeks Later

You feel a little better and are going around the apartment ridding yourself of things that remind you of Fjalar. You throw out the novelty snow globe of Iceland he gave you for Christmas that's just filled to the brim with snow, as well as the cookbook *1001 Easy and Fun Eel Dishes for Every Saint's Day*. You consider throwing away the headphones, but they were so expensive you hate to do it. You remember Fjalar had a set he used to play some online fighting troll game called "World of Warcraft" or something. You have the equipment; you might as well give it a shot.

Six Weeks Later

You're really enjoying "World of Warcraft." You've developed a character named Ravenwater who is an elfin assassin. This apparently means that she can hide in small spaces and likes to stab people with little or no provocation, but because she's an elf she tends to use cute, glittery little edged weapons.

Eight Weeks Later

While prowling the outskirts of the castle keep one fine midsummer's eve, you meet a wayfarer with the username Fjalar_Iceland_Cod. You sneak up behind his character and stab him in the nuts so hard he explodes. *That's what it feels like, Fjalar.*

Create a Family Tree

You've been obsessed with genealogy ever since you fell asleep watching an episode of *Are You Being Served?* on BBC America, woke up, and couldn't find the remote control to change the now playing *Who Do You Think You Are?* marathon. After searching high and low for the remote (read: haphazardly patting around the folds of your duvet and sighing heavily), you came to the harsh realization that one of two things was going to have to happen: you were either going to have to physically get up to change the channel, or spend the next hour learning all about Sarah Jessica Parker's rich German ancestry. It was a Sophie's Choice of epic proportions, but (as is typically the case) laziness won and a fascination with your own lineage was born. After months of interviewing relatives and collecting family documents, you sit down and are finally ready to make your very own family tree.

One Day Later

After confirming with your grandmother that yes, Virginia, there is a Juda-Claus—and this year for Hanukkah he brought you one-sixteenth of a Jewish identity, you decide to fully immerse yourself in Jewish culture to reconnect with your roots.

Seven Days Later

You insist on gathering the family for Shabbat dinner, at the end of which, you blow out the candle and make a wish.

One Month Later

You throw yourself a bat mitzvah at Dave and Buster's where you read aloud from Fran Drescher's cancer memoir, *Cancer Schmancer*, and ride the *Star Wars* flight simulator until you puke.

Two Months Later

"You call this rugelach? Moishe's on Second Avenue between Sixth and Seventh—*that* is rugelach."

Three Months Later

So moved by your newfound faith, you are, that you decide to go on a birthright trip to Israel so you can gain a deeper appreciation for your heritage and *re*-reconnect with your Jewish identity.

Six Months Later

On your first day there, *just* as your handsome Israeli tour guide, Avi, offers to give you a boost onto your camel, the clouds part, trumpets blare, and Jesus Christ gloriously descends down to Earth. He takes one look at you, scoffs, and says, "Shoulda stuck with the Lutherans, girlie." Well, at least he has that Jewish sense of humor.

Assign *Sex and the City* Characters to Your Friends

Birthdays rarely work out for a woman with impulse control as poor as yours. Two years ago you went to New Orleans, did sixteen tequila shots, and staggered around Tulane's campus screaming *"I'm Tropical Storm Drunk!"* The next year, in a failed attempt to take it down a notch, you went to Atlantic City and got banned from the buffet for filling your purse with crab puffs. This year, you opted for a nice old-fashioned slumber party with your three best girlfriends. It was fun to begin with, but after a while you began to realize that, yes, thirty-something women were playing "Truth or Dare" in polyester negligees, and yes, the last dare involved a home equity loan. To spice things up, you decide to try something you read in a magazine, and decide among yourselves which of your friends most closely resembles which character from the cast of *Sex and the City*. Were you dowdy, pedantic Miranda; I-don't-believe-for-a-second-she's-articulate-enough-to-be-a-writer Carrie; graying trollop Samantha; or we-need-a-fourth-woman-space-filler Charlotte? Somehow, this led to hurt feelings.

 ### Five Minutes Later
No one is speaking to each other.

Ten Minutes Later
Everyone has left, and you're beginning to get text messages along the lines of "Can you believe her! Can you believe what she said! So angry :(!" This is not your best birthday, but it's not your worst by a fairly wide margin.

Three Days Later

You're getting tired of moderating this catfight. You've spent the last seventy-two hours dispensing bromides like "She doesn't think you're a whore, she's just jealous of how in touch with your body you are" and "She didn't say you were unattractive, what she meant is that your beauty lies in your strength." Even Oprah wouldn't dare spout that last one, but you're tired and your game is off. Finally, you tell each of them that if they're not happy, they should get off the phone for five minutes and make some changes, starting with not being such a damn whineasaurus.

Five Days Later

Changes were made, all right. The group's "Charlotte," convinced her characterization meant she was boring, robbed a convenience store with a cricket bat; startlingly enough, it was apparently her third strike.

Six Days Later

"Miranda," who felt she was being called ugly, decided to update her look with a *perm* of all things, and now looks exactly like her own mother did in 1984.

Seven Days Later

"Samantha," protesting that she is not a slut, married her gynecologist. It's commitment, of a sort.

Eight Days Later

You realize you were lucky to be the Carrie; American womanhood has done better than Sarah Jessica Parker in a tiara and chartreuse silk clamdiggers, but it's also done a lot worse.

Write Fan Mail

After locking yourself in your apartment and watching nine glorious back-to-back hours of the fantastically underrated mid-'90s animated series *The Critic*, you feel a newfound love and respect for its star, voice actor Jon Lovitz. His impeccable comedic timing. His sensuous baritone. The way a sweater vest hugs his delicate animated frame *just so*. You wonder if he still gets fan mail. You hope so. Actually, that gives you an idea!

One Hour Later

After spraying the letter with some Tommy Girl and kissing it once for luck, you send it off to his agent in L.A. and already feel cosmically connected to him.

One Week Later

As you flip through the usual contents of the day's mail (Omaha Steaks catalog, bill, overdraft notice, bill) you're shocked to see a return address label bearing the Lovitz family crest and immediately tear open the letter. Jon Lovitz was so touched by your fan mail that he not only took the time to personally write you back, but also included a four-by-six color print of him and Kevin Nealon hanging out on the set of 2000's *Little Nicky* with "just goofin—1999" written on the back.

Two Weeks Later

You combine the framed photograph, a Hawaiian shirt you won on eBay supposedly once worn by Lovitz on the set of *Trapped in Paradise*, and a votive candle to create a makeshift shrine for the actor above your washing machine. You pray to it before meals and swear it has mystical healing powers.

One Month Later

You decide to take things to the next level and fly out to his Hollywood home to "observe" him from the bushes across the street.

One Month and Two Hours Later

While taking the trash out one night, Lovitz recognizes you from the numerous photos you've sent him of yourself emptying the dishwasher in the nude, and he invites you in for dinner. It's exciting at first, but there's really only so long you can push around paella with your fork and listen to anecdotes about Tia Carrere's drinking problem on the set of *High School High* before you yawn, look at your watch, and tell him you should really be getting back to your bush. After giving him the slip, you ultimately decide that the obsession has lost its mystique and it's time to pack it in and go back home.

One Month and Eighteen Hours Later

As you walk into your house, tired from the long flight, you're shocked to see Jon Lovitz sitting at your kitchen table with a fresh pot of coffee and a copy of *City Slickers II: The Legend of Curly's Gold* ready to go. "I took the Red Eye!" he exclaims as he gives a hearty double-thumbs up and suggestively winks. Looks like the tables have turned.

Join Facebook

After years of resisting, you've finally decided to give in and join Facebook. Not necessarily because you want to be part of the fad, mind you, but because someone you went to college with converted to Zoroastrianism and is going on trial for attempted murder, and now you're wondering what the rest of the gang is up to. You've created an account, uploaded a recent photo of yourself (the one where your brother's shoulder is in the foreground and blocks a good two-out-of-three of your chins, obviously), and are ready to see what all the fuss is about.

Thirty Minutes Later

Huh. You sort of expected everyone you went to high school with to have gained weight, but it appears the exact opposite of that happened. You kind of wish someone had told you that that's the direction they were headed. May have changed something on your end.

Thirty-Five Minutes Later

You're inundated with bizarre requests to join "Vampire Wars," scrabble games, and mah-jongg tournaments from friends you haven't talked to in fifteen years and a girl you felt up once on a couch in college and never saw again. You decide to indulge in the farming simulation game "FarmVille" because it sounds the most Christian.

Two Days Later

This. Shit. Is. *Addictive.*

Two Months Later

Playing FarmVille has effectively taken over your life. You close your eyes at night and all you see are digitized cherry trees and chickens. You break up with your girlfriend of eight years because she refuses to be an enabler and buy you more bales of hay, and your friends aren't talking to you because you've been exploiting them for topiaries. After getting fired for not doing any work in months, you decide to use your severance money to buy an *actual* farm in the English countryside.

Four Months Later

As it turns out, real farming is considerably harder than cyber farming. In real farming you have to get up early, you can't purchase an "unwither" option to rejuvenate your crops, and actual swine are fussy, to say the least. You decide to unwind by playing a little FarmVille. That'll get you into the spirit!

Six Months Later

Because you've been inside playing FarmVille for the past six weeks, your (real) farm goes under, you go bankrupt, and your creditors confiscate your computer.

One Year Later

You start busking for change to buy time at the Internet café to check on your FarmVille. An hour of breakdancing usually gets you enough for a ten-minute planting session. Twelve minutes if the pound is healthy.

Go on a Blind Date

Your best friend's boss asked her if she would set him up with a nice, attractive, young lady (not too prudish) and you instantly jumped to her mind. You're single and sassy and have been looking to get back into the dating game since breaking up with your boyfriend a few months ago. An avid fan of BET's *Hell Date*, you were hesitant to accept the offer, but ultimately decided to go for it when you saw that he looks like a younger, less English John Cleese. Your motto has always been "If they're lanky and snide, they're worth the ride," so you're eager, but also anxious. You start getting ready for your date and decide that you'll have a glass of wine to calm your nerves.

One Hour Later

One glass of wine turns into two, two turn into a bottle, finishing the bottle turns into a shot of Sambuca (for luck), and as you steady your elbows on the table and apply your lipstick with both hands, you realize you might be *slightly* drunker than you meant to be.

Two Hours Later

At the restaurant, you ask the sommelier for three fingers of Dewar's ("and make 'em like, fat guy fingers") and turn to your date and start a rambling and incoherent discourse on . . . actually you don't remember what it was on, but you think it had something to do with art restoration?

Three Hours Later

He walks you home and at your doorway, you heartily pat him three times on the chest, shoot with a finger gun, and tell him he's an "officer and a gentleman." You eventually get your key in the lock and toddle off to bed.

Two Days Later

Your friend is less than thrilled to hear about your "sloppy" behavior and confronts you about what happened on the date. When she over-reacts upon hearing that you drank before the date, you explain that you get drunk before lots of things: dates, hayrides, work—you know, the usual.

One Week Later

Genuinely concerned about your well-being, your friend rallies the troops and surprises you with an intervention. Initially you're dismayed and annoyed, but then when she mentions that everyone's pitched in to send you to Heartstrings Recovery Center in Malibu, California, you decide to fake the shakes and go with it. You could use a paid vacation at the beach.

Three Months Later

Your doctors are so impressed with your "progress" that they nominate you to join the Heartstrings P.A.L.S. (Peers Assisting, Loving, and Supporting) Program. You're shocked to see that your mentee is none other than the crazy, beautiful star of *Crazy/Beautiful*, Kirsten Dunst.

Five Years Later

It's not that you're not supportive, but it would be nice to go one goddamn day without getting a call from Kirsten Dunst saying, "GOTTA HUFF—TALK ME DOWN."

Give Money to a Homeless Person

You have a long history of being a very charitable, selfless, thoughtful person. You still give to NPR, even though you never got that autographed picture of Terry Gross, and you sometimes even leave a *nickel* in the leave-a-penny-take-a-penny jar. For lack of a better word, you are a saint. Still riding high from scratching off three maracas and a poncho on a "Cash Olé!" lottery ticket, you round the corner on your walk home from the office and see Douglas, the homeless man who resides on the subway grate outside The Men's Wearhouse. You've been so blessed, so you hand him a $20 bill and tell him to "stay strong, brother."

One Hour Later

Douglas uses your $20 to go to Value Village and buys a Hemingway-esque cable-knit sweater, a quart of Wild Turkey, a remaindered notebook with a unicorn on the cover, and some pens, then heads to the men's shelter to start writing his riches-to-rags memoir.

Six Months Later

An editor at HarperCollins praises Douglas's manuscript, tentatively titled *Brother, Can You Spare a Rhyme? The Douglas Boone Story in Verse*, as "heartbreaking. This generation's *Tuesdays with Morrie*," and signs him.

One Year Later

Brother, Can You Spare a Rhyme? makes Oprah cry so hard she gets snot all over her Wamsutta throw pillows. She goes on *Ellen* solely to promote the book. The resulting publicity sells a record-breaking number of books and Ron Howard buys the film rights.

Eighteen Months Later

Instead of buying a condo and a sports team, Douglas hires a competent investment analyst to manage his sudden wealth. It's important to avoid the "easy come, easy go" examples of M. C. Hammer and Gary Coleman.

Two Years Later

One of Douglas's newest acquisitions is Solutions Tech, Inc., which owns the Richmond Group, which holds as a subsidiary Glassman and Sons, your employer. He sells the whole mess to a South Korean conglomerate and you're laid off in the resulting restructuring.

Three Years Later

Now you're homeless. Instead of giving you money, some guy gives you a copy of Douglas's inspiring book *Brother, Can you Spare a Rhyme? The Douglas Boone Story in Verse* to motivate you to pull yourself up by the bootstraps. What a prick.

Ask Your Boyfriend for a Pet

Valentine's Day is around the corner and there's only one thing you really want: a teacup rat terrier named "Templeton." You've been subtly dropping hints to your boyfriend, and when that didn't work, you started withholding sex and threatening to key his Honda. On Valentine's night, you sit poised as you hear your boyfriend's keys jangling at the door. You sit on the sofa and nonchalantly read *Redbook*, but inside you're thinking if he doesn't have a puppy and you just spent all that money on Purina, boy is your face gonna be red!

One Minute Later

Your boyfriend walks in the door holding a large box wrapped in pink paper with holes cut in the side. If he's gotten you a lizard as a gag gift you're going to punch him. Squarely in the jaw.

Five Minutes Later

You open the box and discover an adorable teacup rat terrier panting inside. You immediately take Templeton into the bathroom so you can wash off the "travel dust."

Three Hours Later

You've washed Templeton and then followed that up with a hot oil treatment, pedicure, and Swedish massage. Your boyfriend wants to make love to you on Valentine's Day, but you refuse because you think it's important for you and Templeton to bond.

Two Weeks Later

You pay no attention to your boyfriend because you're always brushing, plucking, trimming, and painting various parts of Templeton.

Eventually he packs up the whey powder and hair gel he keeps at your apartment and dumps you saying that you and the dog deserve each other.

Three Months Later

You've spent so much on dog accessories that you're having trouble making rent. You decide to sue your ex-boyfriend for alimony to help support Templeton.

Four Months Later

You bring your case to the only court that would hear it: Judge Judy's Studio of Justice. In a judgment that is a surprise only to you, she declares you "dumb as a bag of hair and spoiled to boot," awards you no alimony, and sentences you to make something of yourself.

Four Months and One Day Later

Judge Judy's no-nonsense tough love really makes you reevaluate your choices. You look into adult education options and are torn between locksmithing, washer/dryer repair, and private investigating. In the end, you decide to combine the best features of each and get your HVAC certification.

Eighteen Months Later

You graduate and are immediately hired by a midsize reputable firm. You write Judge Judy a letter telling her the news and thanking her for putting you on the straight and narrow. She writes back and tells you that she's proud of you and knew that you were a fighter. Best of all, you can now afford to buy Templeton special food for his diabetes.

CHAPTER 4

Facedown in the Punch Bowl

Putting the "Special" Back in Special Occasions

According to Chinese legend, the first calendar was invented by the "Yellow Emperor," Huangdi. A slightly less popular myth holds that he showed his invention to his wife, who recommended that he "zazz up" the calendar by making some of the days "special" somehow: "Make the peasants do weird things on those days. Walk backwards or live for generations on cabbage soup or something." Because the empress was as beautiful as she was a nag, the emperor agreed, and the fateful idea of "doing something on a specific day" was born. In the years that followed, holidays, birthdays, anniversaries, and *Star Wars*–themed freshman mixers all grew out of this basic idea of special days. These special occasions are now so loaded with ritual, emotion, etiquette, and history that even the most minor misstep can bring the whole edifice tumbling down around you—people historically wind up red-faced on red-letter days.

Really Do Oktoberfest Right This Year

One of the most endearing things about Americans is our national tendency to "borrow" drinking holidays from other countries. Mexico won the Battle of Puebla? Let's drink on May 5th! But the jewel in our boozy crown is Oktoberfest, three weeks of constant beer and brat consumption indirectly commemorating the 1810 wedding of a Bavarian prince. This year, you've decided to really get into the spirit and create a special Oktoberfest homebrew for the occasion. You've got a big pot, a bootleg supply of crystal-clear Alpine spring water, some discount grain, and a dream. Time to boil them all together, bottle the result, and sell it to drunks.

Three Weeks Later
The beer is fermented and ready to drink. It's not . . . *good*, per se, but it'll do. You only have a little taste of your own creation, since you want to have a clear head to sell it.

Three Weeks, Three Hours Later
You took your batch of beer to the fairgrounds where the big Oktoberfest kickoff is happening, and it's been selling like 100 proof hotcakes.

Three Weeks, Five Hours Later
Things are getting intense. People are falling to the ground and screaming much earlier in the evening than they ordinarily would. A young woman near you is scratching at her arms with disturbing vigor, and beyond her two men are chasing a "demon" only they can see with a tuba and a soft pretzel. A lot of people are shrieking and swatting at the air wildly, and several have begun to pray. It's not the worst party you've been to.

Three Weeks, Six Hours Later

The situation has gone downhill. Everyone is rolling around on the ground screaming about monsters, divine vengeance, and that awful burning itch. A few of the sufferers have gathered themselves sufficiently to hold a prayer service—as this reaches some kind of climax, one of them points at you and shouts, "Witch! Wiiiitch!" This cannot bode well. They're approaching. . . .

One Year Later

"Indianapolis Witch Trials" (from Wikipedia, the free encyclopedia)

The <u>Indianapolis</u> Witch Trials were a riotlike public disturbance that took place at an <u>Oktoberfest</u> celebration outside Indianapolis. Seven people were killed in mob violence and show trials that took place in one evening; it was later discovered that the perpetrators were hallucinating after having drunk homemade <u>beer</u> tainted with psychoactive <u>ergot</u> fungus, a common grain parasite. The brewer, who told a friend he had bought the grain used in the beer's production from "some discount feed store out in Assholeville," (citation needed) was among the dead.

Draft a Fantasy Football Team

You know it's about to be fall when everyone starts getting excited about their fantasy football team. All over our fair country, men gather, crack open a few brewskis, and discuss Ben Roethlisberger's powerful thighs without seeming "gay." You've got a pretty good lineup this year, provided no one violates his parole. You usually do pretty poorly within your fantasy league, due to your tendency to draft based on "heart" and "stick-to-it-iveness" instead of actual skill, but you've got a feeling this is your year. Here's the kickoff!

One Week Later

The first week of play has not gone well for your team. Donovan McNabb has made a last-minute decision to join the Israeli rugby team this year, just to see how the other half lives. Scott Fujita got his hand stuck in a jar of pickles while reaching for the last one at the bottom and can't play until someone breaks him out. Lance Moore somehow has tetanus, and won't give any details. You're in last place in your league, behind the guy who simply drafted the Cleveland Browns and the guy who didn't understand how to play and drafted Lara Flynn Boyle as his kicker.

Two Weeks Later

You are losing, losing, losing. You could accept the setbacks with grace if only your friend Ray would stop gloating. He keeps talking about how he and "his boy Eli Manning" are going to take it all the way. It's driving you up the wall.

Three Weeks Later

You've reached your breaking point. Eli Manning threw a touchdown pass just now, and Ray got so excited he humped the sofa and spiked an empty beer can into your lap. This will end.

Four Weeks Later

You lurk outside MetLife Stadium with a tire iron. Your plan is simple: run up to Manning when he comes out of practice and give him a solid Tonya Harding–style whack across the knees. He'll be out for the season, Ray will be thwarted, and you might have a shot at third place.

Five Weeks Later

You did manage to scamper up to Eli Manning, who is surprisingly handsome in person, and thwack him in the knee with the tire iron. Unfortunately for you, he was still wearing all of his pads, so you didn't so much "hurt" him as "test his knee protection." You were lucky Eli is a nonviolent guy; you were unlucky that the rest of the Giants' current roster weren't. From your hospital bed, you can barely move your head enough to catch a game on TV. Manning has sent another rocket straight into the end zone. Dammit.

Make a Living Will

You're not as young as you used to be. Your hair is graying, your joints can detect low-pressure systems as far away as Cleveland, and just yesterday you turned off a Rolling Stones album because it was "too loud and jarring." The end isn't quite near yet, but it's certainly closer than it used to be. You don't want your family to have to make hard decisions about your care while they're already upset over your medical condition, and you also want to make sure you receive the care you deserve. You decide that the considerate course of action, both for your loved ones and your future self, is to take the time now to make some uncomfortable decisions about your end-of-life care.

One Week Later

During your annual checkup, you broach the subject with your primary care physician. Working from the list of questions you drew up last night after doing some light Internet research, you ask her what you can expect in the event you are unable to make your own medical decisions. She answers as well as she can while sticking to generalities and invites you to help yourself to any pamphlets in the waiting area.

Two Weeks Later

You meet with your minister and discuss moral and ethical issues surrounding the subject of a living will. He gives you the Episcopal Church's official stance, but also talks with you about your personal beliefs before praying with you.

Three Weeks Later

Now that you understand the medical situation and have considered how your faith affects this decision, you have your attorney draw up the papers. You read them over carefully and ask for several clarifications before signing them.

Four Weeks Later

You call your wife and eldest child into the living room and tell them that you've made some preparations in the event you are seriously ill or injured, and that there's no need to discuss particulars now, but all the papers are in your top left desk drawer, in a manila envelope marked "private and confidential."

Thirty-Six Years Later

As you succumb to heart disease, sadly still the number one killer of Americans, your family's burden of grief is lightened by the fact that they know exactly what your final wishes are. Free from guilt and uncertainty, they are able to spend your wake joyfully celebrating a life well lived and swapping cherished stories of your humor, heart, and good old-fashioned horse sense. It seemed like a good idea to make a living will—and it was.

Wait Until the Last Minute to Do Your Taxes

You always have a hard time remembering when your income tax filing is due. You know it's sometime around Passover, but Passover was late this year and all of a sudden it was April 14th, and you had but a few short hours to get your paperwork in order. You figure it can't be that hard; anything that literally *everyone* in the country has to do can't have too steep of a learning curve. You took AP calculus in high school, and damn near passed it, too. You break out the old graphic calculator, crack open a Bud Light, and sit down with the shoebox marked "Receipts and etc., misc.," ready to go.

One Hour Later

Wait. Net? Gross? This isn't even English!

Nine Hours Later

Midnight strikes, and you're still at your table trying to figure out if you can claim your iguana as a dependent. You finally stuff everything into a manila envelope, give it a couple of spritzes of Old Spice so you'll seem sophisticated, and drop it off at the post office. You're sure they'll tell you if you made a mistake.

Three Weeks Later

You receive an ominous-looking letter from the IRS. It is addressed to "Draft-Dodging Tax-Evading Pinko" and contains a picture of Uncle Sam holding a weeping Statue of Liberty, captioned "Now look what you've gone and done. You've made your mother cry." Faced with something the letter refers to as a "double-fisted, full-bore audit," you panic,

feed the iguana, microwave all your credit cards and
passport, and skip town.

Two Months Later

You've decided the best way to avoid the audit and inevitable incar-
ceration and "first dance" with your cellmate is to go to Idaho and try
to drop off the grid. You find a secluded patch of land, build a service-
able lean-to shelter, and use the last of your cash to buy beef jerky and
tomato seeds so you can move toward self-sufficiency.

Two Months, One Week Later

The "secluded spot" you set yourself up on turns out to be a privately
owned KOA campground. You are discovered by the owner and arrested
for trespassing, which leads to the IRS finding you. You are tried for tax
evasion and "general chickenshittery" and sentenced to five years. Your
cellmate has no interest in a forced romance, but insists on playing end-
less rounds of poker. Since you're as bad with pretend money as you are
with real money, you always lose.

Throw a Surprise Party

You pride yourself on being a good friend, but you really shit the bed earlier this year. You completely forgot your best friend's birthday—to be fair, it's the day after St. Patty's and you weren't thinking particularly clearly, but you should have left a note for yourself. You apologized profusely, but Jackie kept saying, "No, it's fine!" in that high-pitched "I'm still pissed" voice, so you knew you had to make up for it somehow, and then you had an idea. Everyone expects a surprise party on their birthday, but how many people get one on their *half*-birthday? Jackie turns twenty-eight *and a half* tonight, and you've gathered all her friends into her house to wait for her. You're all hidden and waiting, and then the doorbell rings. . . .

One Minute Later

Oh, crap. It's the pizza guy. If Jackie sees him, the cover is blown. You grab him by the arm and yank him inside while everyone hides again.

Four Minutes Later

Pizza Guy is yammering about his Eleventh Amendment rights and threatening to call the police and his shift manager. You try to explain that the Eleventh Amendment lays the foundation for sovereign immunity and that he probably means the Fourth Amendment, prohibiting unlawful search and seizure, and also that he's ruining the surprise. He will have none of it, so you snatch away his phone, strong-arm him into the utility room, and lock him in.

Six Hours Later

The party was a blast. Jackie had a great time, everyone had lots of laughs, and you consider it a total success. You suddenly remember you forgot to let the Pizza Guy out of the utility room. When you open the door he pounces on you and tries to choke you, snarling through his gritted teeth that now all the pizzas in his truck are *ruined* because they've just been sitting out there. You gasp that a lot of people like stale pizza better than fresh, but he keeps choking you. You manage to grab the iron and hit him in the head with it, and he goes down like a sack of beans.

Seven Hours Later

You knew there was a reason Jackie was your best friend, even if she gets passive-aggressive when you forget her birthday. She helps you load the Pizza Guy's corpse into his truck, and follows you to the abandoned quarry. After you push the truck containing Pizza Guy in and watch it sink under the black water, she drives you home, stopping on the way for ice cream.

Forty Years Later

Jackie backed up your alibi and the Pizza Guy's disappearance was never solved. You had to defend yourself, you know, but you still feel guilty—and sometimes, when you're completely alone, you smell the strong and unmistakable odor of a large cheese pie with peppers and Canadian bacon.

Renew Your Driver's License

Like most people, you've always been self-conscious of your driver's license photo, in which you sport a three-day beard and a sweat-stained Aerosmith T-shirt. Now that your license is about to expire, you've decided to take the most flattering, least embarrassing, best-groomed borderline glamour shot you can. You bleach your teeth, get a haircut, and have a "gentleman's facial." You arrive at the DMV freshly shaven, in a nice suit, and—your little secret—wearing colored contacts to make your eyes an especially sparkling blue. You fill out the forms, stand on the line, and say "Cheese!" as the woman snaps your photograph. This must be how Bruce Willis feels *every single day.*

One Hour Later

You speed home, hoping a hot lady cop will pull you over and look at your extremely handsome driver's license, but no luck.

Four Hours Later

You pull your new license out of your wallet to admire it again. God *damn.* Who is that sexy piece of meat? You notice, to your surprise, that the woman at the DMV has made an error and coded your license as veteran status. You consider going back and having it fixed, but you don't want to risk having to retake the picture. You're not really used to the contacts and your eyes are all red.

Eight Days Later

You are carded while buying beer at the convenience store. The clerk sees your "veteran status" and gives you the beer for free, throws in a York Peppermint Patty, and thanks you for your service. He seems so glad to do this that you hate to explain the truth, and you're really looking forward to the refreshing blast you'll get from the candy.

Three Months Later

Crime is a slippery slope. After you got the free beer and candy, you started claiming to be a veteran to get all kinds of perks, including discounted movie tickets, six free months of satellite TV, and half-priced lap dances down at the Slippery Whisker. You get caught when, one day over pinochle at the VFW, someone asks what unit you were with and you panic and say "Gryffindor."

Six Months Later

You plead no contest to charges of impersonating a veteran. The judge, a believer in creative sentencing, orders you to do a tour of duty in Iraq.

Three Years Later

Iraq was as you expected: sand, with occasional explosions. On the bright side, when you get back you will legitimately qualify for veteran discounts!

Celebrate Earth Day

You've had to confront an inconvenient truth about yourself—you are a freakishly wasteful human being. Sometimes when you can't sleep, you turn on the shower for white noise. You prefer to make four or five passes with the toilet paper just to be sure, and when you go camping you surround your tent with a hazy cloud of aerosol room spray because you like to *see* the forest but *smell* the beach. You never cared about your "carbon footprint" before, but last night you accidentally caught a particularly moving Earth Day PSA in which Suzanne Somers fed a baby tiger and delivered a dire warning about climate change. If there was room for the three of them in that little apartment on *Three's Company*, surely there's enough room on this planet for all of God's creatures. You decided to start with Somers's first suggestion, and replace all the light bulbs in your house with the new energy-efficient ones. You load up on new bulbs at the hardware store, and get ready to be the change you want to see in the world.

Two Hours Later

You've replaced all the bulbs in your house with the new "green" ones except for the ones in the dining room chandelier. The chandelier is on a short chain and the ceiling is very high, so you have to balance a step stool on a chair on the phone book to be able to reach it. Inevitably, the stool slips, you grab at the chandelier, and wind up hanging about fifteen feet above the hard tile floor. It's uncomfortable, but you're not too worried. Your date will get worried when you don't show up at the Cracker Barrel and come rescue you.

Five Hours Later

Your house phone rings, and your answering machine picks up. "Josh? This is Alison. I'm not really interested in your excuse for standing me up this time. I'm sure you've prepared a great story about car trouble and vampires, but save it for the next cute waitress you give a 40 percent tip."

Nine Hours Later

You decide to go ahead and fall, try to tuck and roll, and just accept the injuries, but you've been clutching the chandelier so hard your muscles have locked into place. Sometime in the night you pass out.

Sixteen Hours Later

Weak from pain, fatigue, and dehydration, you are only dimly aware of your cleaning lady's entrance. She shrieks and runs to the phone. You hear her call 911 and give a rambling explanation that prominently features the words *"el señor"* and *"asfixia autoerotica."* You can't decide whether to give her a raise for saving you or fire her for assuming you get off hanging from light fixtures, so you call it even.

Go as Something Unusual for Halloween

You're constantly unprepared for holidays. Last year for Valentine's Day you got your girlfriend scratch-offs, condoms, and a frozen pizza from the Texaco across the street from her apartment, and you've never given a gift that wasn't wrapped in yesterday's newspaper (often featuring a partly filled-out word scramble). Hoping to avoid a repeat of last year's hastily thrown together heavy eyeliner + business suit = "slutty Alan Greenspan" Halloween costume, you started brainstorming costume ideas in April, and by June you had decided to go as Anubis, jackal-headed Egyptian god of the dead. Halloween night has finally rolled around and you can't wait to debut your costume at your friend's party. One last check in the mirror: linen loincloth hanging right? Check. Bare torso oiled up? Check. Papier-mâchéd dog head on securely? Check. Time to make some Halloween magic.

Five Minutes Later

As you walk to your friend's house, you realize that it's the middle of fall and sixteen ounces of baby oil does not a Northface jacket make.

Fifteen Minutes Later

You've been at the party for five minutes and have already had to explain your costume to everyone there, except for one guy who thinks you're the Boston University terrier and keeps shouting "TERRIER PRIDE!" at you from across the party. You don't have the heart to tell him you went to Tufts.

An Hour Later

Halloween being what it is, you start hitting on a woman in a lioness costume. She tells you she's Nala from *The Lion King* and lives down the street. Bingo.

Eleven Hours Later

You wake up the next morning and survey your unfamiliar surroundings. Anime posters line the walls; a sketchbook lies open to a drawing of a younger, strangely muscular Garfield; and *Zoobilee Zoo* plays softly on the TV in the background. It's no *Playboy* mansion, but "Nala" is still a solid seven in the morning, so you wake her up and ask her to meet you for breakfast after you run home and change.

Twelve Hours Later

You walk into Denny's and are surprised to see "Nala" freshly showered and made up, yet still wearing kitten ears and the cat-eye contacts from last night. Considering you're secretly wearing last night's loincloth underneath your basketball shorts *(it breathes so well!)*, it doesn't seem that weird and you join her.

Twelve Hours and Thirty Minutes Later

As she laps up the leftover milk from her cereal bowl with her tongue, it starts to get weird. Suddenly it dawns on you why she hissed at you last night when you stepped on her costume's tail.

Twelve Hours and Thirty-One Minutes Later

Before you have time to run away as fast as your *two* legs will carry you, your friends walk in. They see you. They see her. You see them. And suddenly everyone knows.

Fifty Years Later

Your friends still give you shit about that Halloween you went home with a Furry.

Tell the Waiter It's Your Friend's Birthday

It's one of the oldest tricks in the book. You and friend Pam have just finished a meal of Jalapeño Kickers and Asian Glazed Salmon at Ruby Tuesday's, when she excuses herself to go to the bathroom. You don't know if it's the three "Strong Island" Iced Teas or RuTues' anything-goes attitude talking, but tonight you're feeling a little mischievous. Your waiter, Chad, comes over to take your empty plates and suddenly, you get a genius idea. "Just so you know," you whisper, eyes anxiously darting back and forth between him and the restrooms, "today is my friend's birthday, so if you could do a little something special for her, that would be great." Chad's eyes immediately light up. He's been waiting for this all night. He knows *just* what to do. With an all-knowing wink, Chad whisks away your plates just as Pam returns from the bathroom. Good thing she peed first. . . .

One Minute Later

You can barely contain yourself. Because he thinks it's her—And she doesn't know he—But you said it was—And OHHHHHH, what a farce!

Three Minutes Later

In parade formation, Chad and the rest of the Ruby Tuesday's crew wind their way through the restaurant, stop at your table, and launch into a full-throated rendition of "The Ruby Tuesday's Birthday Blow-Out Rag." They're all running a little sharp, but they brought with them a complimentary hot fudge sundae.

Five Minutes Later

Adequately embarrassed, Pam starts shoveling sundae into her mouth like a gravedigger on a deadline. She always was a "healthy eater."

Six Minutes Later

A rogue peanut flies to the back of her throat and lodges itself sideways. Not even the vigorous pumping of Chad's (surprisingly toned) arms can clear her airways and she dies as she lived—fast, hard, and full of chocolate.

Six Months Later

You've been seeing a psychiatrist but nothing helps. You're still wracked with guilt and birthdays give you panic attacks. One night while watching *The Jacksons: An American Dream* during an all-too-common bout of insomnia, you think you've found the answer when circa "Dancing Machine" Michael explains that he's never had a birthday party because he and his family are Jehovah's Witnesses. Now we're cookin' with gas!

Nine Months Later

Being a Jehovah's Witness has turned your life around. It's like God is a cool kid and you're finally sitting at his table. You're happy to evangelize door-to-door for people who have done so much for you, and you're headed out to the new subdivision east of town to save a few more souls before lunch. Unfortunately, the Mormons have already staked that patch, and you ignite a bloody turf war referred to by CNN as "The What the Fucks? vs. The What the Hells?"

Five Years Later

Jaden Smith plays you in a movie about the conflict called, *Utah Burning.* His performance is widely panned as "wooden and lacking depth."

Take a Mental Health Day

You had no idea working at Barnes and Noble would be this exhausting. Your cigarette breaks are too short to enjoy an entire Newport, you can't keep enough copies of *Eat, Pray, Love* on the shelf, and not a day goes by that a girl wearing combat boots and a babydoll dress doesn't come in to complain about not having the newest issue of *Bitch*. You would literally rather wash down a handful of tacks with a bottle of Boone's Farm than show up for your shift today, so you smoke a few dozen Newports for that raspy authenticity, call your boss, and fake a vicious case of laryngitis to stay home. You feel guilty until you see there's a *Just Shoot Me* marathon on and you break out a pint of rocky road. This is just what the doctor ordered.

Two Hours Later

Wendie Malick is one of the most underrated comedic geniuses of our time.

Four Hours Later

As you flip through the channels, you catch one of those blank screens with the message "This film has been formatted to fit your television screen." You cross your fingers and hope for a winner. Suddenly Anne Ramsey in a black Jeep Cherokee goes flying across the screen and you realize you've just rolled double sixes: It's *Goonies*. From the very beginning. You are officially living the dream.

Five Hours Later

Your wife threatens to divorce you when you won't help bring in the groceries from the car until she does the "Truffle Shuffle." You concede, but still kind of think it would have been worth it.

Six Hours Later

The movie ends, leaving you feeling oddly inspired. You decide to dig for buried treasure in the back yard. You probably won't find a treasure map or chest full of jewels, but you might find a coffee can filled with twenties leftover from the '80s savings and loan crisis.

Eight Hours Later

While digging in the backyard, you accidentally hit a gas main and blow you, your house, and your '94 Chevy Malibu to smithereens. You barely have time to shout, "Goonies never say die!"

Two Months Later

After conducting a thorough investigation of the explosion, the FBI decides that no one is so stupid to just dig into a gas main and that your explosion must have been a failed terrorist attack. Your siblings are all forced to change their last name and you join the underwear bomber on the Terrorism Blooper Reel.

Get a Seasonal Part-Time Job

In the end, you have only yourself to blame. You spent the entire fall gorging on candy apples, and the combination of concentrated sugar and constant pulling has done a number on your teeth. You went to the dentist and found out that you're going to need about $5,000 worth of work done. You asked your dentist if insurance would cover it and he laughed so hard he had to lean on the X-ray machine, then patted you affectionately on the knee and handed you a card for a plasma donation center. Unfortunately, your recent cartilage piercing puts the kibosh on that strategy, so you decide to go to the mall and scout out some seasonal part-time retail work.

One Day Later

You consider asking for an application at Pacific Sunwear, but it appears their cutoff age is twenty-three. Armani Exchange is next door, but unfortunately you're not a slender gay Asian man with a passion for fashion. After being turned away at Pier 1 for telling the manager you can "sell the shit out of all of this wicker," you get hired on the spot at Abercrombie & Fitch thanks to the fact that your damaged teeth have put you on an inadvertent diet that has pulled your normally serene features into a persistent bitch face.

Two Weeks Later

While rolling up a mannequin's skinny jeans one day at work, the massive amounts of A&F Eau de Waifstorm circulating through the air system sends you into acute respiratory distress.

One Month Later

Abercrombie & Fitch convinces you to drop your lawsuit by offering you an office job at their headquarters in New Albany, Ohio. You have to really think about it, because it's Ohio, but your horoscope said to take life by the horns, so you decide to accept.

Two Months Later

You arrive for your first day and they put you to work writing offensive T-shirt slogans. You're a little hesitant at first, but after a couple belts of Maker's Mark, you come up with a few gems: "Gay? That's Kind of Gross"; "Young, Dumb, and Full of Egg Foo Young"; and the ever straightforward "Fat Girls Put Out." Your copywriting is a hit around the office.

Three Months Later

You get cocky and push the envelope with a rugby shirt bearing the phrase "Liquor Is Quicker, But Rohypnol Is Quick Y'all!" You are given a pink slip that simply says "Not cool."

Six Months Later

You manage to parlay your experience into a job writing slogan T-shirts at Target. It pays the bills, but it doesn't really challenge you as an artist.

Welcome Spring

The snow has melted, the landscape is green, and the smell of gardenias lazily wafts through the sweet, warm air—spring has sprung. After months of being cooped up in your Montreal home hunkered down against the harsh Canadian winter, you are more than ready to welcome spring into the world and into your heart. You decide the best way to do this is to hang a bird feeder in your backyard to welcome home all the little songbirds on the way back from their southern migration. Welcome home, friends. Welcome home.

One Week Later

You've spent the last week using your antique slingshot to pick off all those goddamn squirrels that have been getting into the bird feeder.

One Month Later

Every morning after you rise, you go out to the bird feeder in your gauzy nightdress, stretch out your arms, sing a little song, and invite our feathered friends to perch on you for a moment of fellowship.

Six Weeks Later

One morning as you bask in the embrace of your winged brethren and join them in a song, a little finch sneezes directly into your open mouth.

Seven Weeks Later

You've been run-down and listless for the past week, so you go to the doctor. He asks if you've done anything unusual recently and you answer, "Oh, nothing out of the ordinary. Going to work, doing laundry, and spending time by my bird feeder." When you mention the birdfeeder, the doctor turns pale, excuses himself, and runs out of the room, locking the door behind him.

Two Months Later

You've been diagnosed with Avian Flu and put in quarantine for three weeks until it runs its course (or you die). You spend the entire time locked in an eight-by-ten cell alone, watching daytime TV and teaching yourself needlepoint.

Two Months and Three Weeks Later

You're finally released from quarantine. The whole experience was traumatizing and you have become fixated on germs and cleanliness. After pouring a gallon of Lysol over the bird feeder, you lock yourself inside and coat all the exterior walls with Saran Wrap. That'll keep those bastards out.

Six Years Later

You've been inside all this time. It's just not safe out there, what with the pope being a Freemason and the liberal media putting anthrax in the drinking water.

Eleven Years Later

You and your eccentricities have become well-known thanks to your many letters to the editor of *Reader's Digest* and a Lifetime biopic is made about your life. It's a good thing you don't pay much attention to the outside world because Valerie Bertinelli phones in a halfhearted performance.

Go to a President's Day Sale

SAVINGS! SAVINGS! SAVINGS! After 364 days of waiting, it's finally President's Day. You'd like to think that if Lincoln were alive today, he'd be freeing you from high prices, because you cannot tell a lie, you really like saving. You're ready to head out to the President's Day sale at the furniture outlet and really clean up. (Something in cherrywood, maybe? For your log cabin?) Your motto when shopping is speak softly and carry a big purse. You vow that there will be no bargain left behind. *Yes we can* buy quality furniture for less and *hope* for *change* in our home's appearance for the better!

Two Hours Later
You leave the furniture warehouse full of more presidential puns and a lovely new sofa.

Two Hours and Thirty Minutes Later
You get the sofa home but can't seem to get it through your front door. You decide to leave it on the porch until you figure out what to do.

One Day Later
Even if you can't get it through the door yet, you're still going to enjoy your lovely new sofa. You pour yourself a glass of Turning Leaf Chardonnay, grab your copy of *Ender's Game*, and plop yourself down on the couch to start getting it broken in.

One Week Later

The weather is so delightful you decide to bring out the TV and a touch lamp for when it gets dark.

Two Weeks Later

This is just as cozy as can be! But you know what would make it even cozier? A mini-fridge and an oriental rug.

One Month Later

By now you've moved a fair amount of your house onto your porch and you're loving it. You get to be outside but have your stuff! It's the best of both worlds! Your neighbors, however, have started to complain to the Homeowner's Association that your house has become an eyesore. They think this is an eyesore? You'll show them.

One Month and One Day Later

You've picked up a dozen or so unused high-flow toilets from the dump and have arranged them on your lawn. When the mood takes you, you fire off a shot at one from your .38. The piles of shattered porcelain certainly make a statement.

Five Years Later

Most of your neighbors have moved away and been replaced with meth addicts, the property value of your house has collapsed, and it's not really as safe as it used to be, but dammit, those toilet-shootin', TV-watchin', great outdoors evenings are what our forefathers fought and died for.

Fail to Beware the Ides of March

Your friend has come up with a wonderful idea for a theme party: an Ides of March toga party. A *Julius Caesar* nerd since tenth-grade English class, you can't wait to don a toga, make a garland out of a bent coat hanger and an ivy that was sick anyway, and party like it's 99 . . . B.C. Some people might say it's in poor taste for a grown woman to dress up in a sheet and celebrate an assassination, but . . . well, they would be right, but if stumbling around in a beer-drenched toga is wrong, you don't want to be right.

Two Weeks Later

Oh shit, the Ides of March is on the *15th?* You could have sworn it was the 17th because of daylight savings or leap year or something weird. You grab the first sheet you see in the linen closet and are still wrapping it around yourself on the way out the door.

Two Weeks and Thirty Minutes Later

Before doing a keg stand, you announce to the assembled company: "Friends, Romans, countrymen—lend me your *beers!*" and are quite pleased with yourself.

Two Weeks and Thirty-Five Minutes Later

Your best friend's boyfriend quietly takes you aside and tells you that you have something on your toga. You look down, see a large red stain on your upper thigh and realize that you accidentally grabbed the sheet with a giant period stain on it.

Two Weeks and Thirty-Six Minutes Later

Sensing your mortification, your best friend's boyfriend hurries you into the bathroom and closes the door. He rummages through the hamper, brings out a denim jacket, and suggests you tie it around your waist. You refuse because it would be historically inaccurate. With an eye roll, he starts looking through a cabinet and pulls out a stain stick. He starts dabbing the blotch on your toga and tells you the stain's coming right out and he doesn't think anyone else saw. You regret telling your best friend you thought he looked like Matthew Perry with a lazy eye when they first started dating.

Two Weeks and Fifty Minutes Later

You walk out of the bathroom ready for a beer and a laugh and the room goes silent. "Et tu, Brute?" your best friend asks, her teeth clenched in fury. You realize you've been missing from the party for about twenty minutes, only to reemerge from the bathroom with your best friend's boyfriend in tow. In addition, the blob of off-white gel on the edge of your toga seems unfortunately suggestive. Blinded by fury and unwilling to listen to your exclamations, your best friend darts into the kitchen and returns holding an enormous knife. With a cry, she lunges forward and stabs you and her boyfriend. She then delivers a lengthy declamation on loyalty and betrayal before turning the knife on herself. On your dying breath, you explain that what she's done here is really more of a Greek tragedy.

CHAPTER 5

When the Wheel of Fortune Runs Over Your Foot

A Grab Bag of Stupid Choices

Until now, you've seen aspects of life in which one can easily imagine a good idea going south. *Of course* your Matt LeBlanc tattoo seems silly after *Joey* only lasted for one season. *Of course* you shouldn't have dated that girl who thought she'd been an alligator in a past life. Relationships are always minefields, the human body is consistently accident-prone, and holidays are nerve-racking for all except the very young and the expertly medicated. You know to be on your lookout in these situations. That said, some days the Fates pick up the cards they use to tell men's destinies and throw them in the air with a giddy "Whee!" so they can play a rousing game of Cosmic 52 Pickup. With this in mind, here's a "wild card" chapter, illustrating what can happen when you're quietly going about your business, and the universe is quietly going nuts.

Do Some Art Modeling

As clichés go, "step out of your comfort zone!" is one of the most insidious. It used to be confined to method actors, who used it as code for "roles where you look like shit are Oscar bait," and nonprofit organization workers, who used it as code for "go to an inner-city neighborhood." Since these two groups are notoriously talkative, the idea spread, and now no one feels comfortable unless they're uncomfortable, and you're no exception. So when you saw an ad seeking "Art Models—All Types Wanted," you decided to give it a whirl. Being naked in front of a dozen art students is a respectable first step into the shallow end of public nudity: If you like it, you can work your way up to streaking the Rose Bowl; if you don't, you can step out of your comfort zone in some other direction and take a pottery class or become a lipstick lesbian. You answer the ad, make an appointment, and prepare to throw caution and garments to the wind.

One Minute Later
Haha! You're totally naked in front of these art kids. There's something oddly powerful about it. You are just *naked*. Nude. Unclothed. Naked. Just as nature intended.

Five Minutes Later
You would love to know the etiquette about farting because a situation is a-*brewin'*.

One Week Later
You've been back to the modeling studio every day this week. You feel oddly free just sitting around naked, and the art students don't even seem to notice when you do a "one cheek sneak." One of them

seems to be developing a crush on you—he makes a fair amount of eye contact and smiles a lot.

Two Months Later

You're a regular down at the studio now. You've been drawn naked, naked on a settee, naked eating a cheeseburger, naked balancing your checkbook, naked except for a giant foam finger that says GO 49ERS, and naked in a series of whimsical wigs. The only sad part is that the little artist who had a crush on you left to take a job doing medical illustrations.

Four Months Later

A woman stops you on the street to tell you how much she admires your courage. You write it off as the David Lynch Moment of the Day.

Five Months Later

It keeps happening. Women keep stopping you on the street, telling you you're strong, then smiling and pressing your hand. It's unnerving.

Seven Months Later

During a routine visit to the gynecologist, you pick up some pamphlets to browse while you wait. With a start, you recognize the woman on "Heavy Periods: What You Can Do." It's *you.* A quick flip through the stack reveals that your artist friend turned medical illustrator has made you the face of heavy periods, endometriosis, uterine cysts, something called "nervous cervix," and "Vaginal Itching: Common Causes."

Seventy Years Later

Sociology textbooks note that art featuring the winsome, smiling "heavy period lady" (model unknown) has helped women confront their medical issues without fear or shame. You don't care very much because you are dead.

Buy a House

It's possible that, hidden in the depths of the Vatican, there exists a bigger buzzkill than your landlord, but you wouldn't bet on it. Every time you have an idea to make your apartment building a more exciting, more appealing place, it gets vetoed with a frown and a condescending phrase. Foosball table in the lobby? "You're too old to get decorating tips from *Animal House*." Life-size display of Santa and his reindeer on the roof? "It might offend residents who aren't Christian, or aren't blind." Performance art in elevators? "I will personally subsidize the cost of concealed handgun permits for the other residents." Well, fine. If he wants to be a sourpuss, let him. You've been saving for a Ms. Pac-Man machine, but that money can just as easily go toward the down payment on your own house, where reindeer are welcome *whenever*.

One Week Later

A three-story Queen Anne *with crown molding* for $40,000? Sold!

Two Months Later

Literally *every* neighbor you've introduced yourself to has slammed the door in your face, started reciting the rosary, or begged you on bended knee to leave before it's too late. They must have a bad problem with charity canvassers in the neighborhood.

Three Months Later

Hmmm. According to a pamphlet put out by the town chamber of commerce, the house you now live in was the site of the infamous "Belligerent Bridesmaid" murders, and is now supposedly haunted by the ghosts of a bride who didn't understand that being a bridesmaid is a lot of work, a bridesmaid who actually looked good in the dress, and two handsy groomsmen who "just kind of assumed . . . you know, it's a wedding. . . ."

Four Months Later

Your attempts to contact the ghosts via Ouija board fail; all it spells out is "LOL" and you can't swear you didn't do that yourself out of boredom. It occurs to you that there might be some fun and money in this alleged haunting. If you really play it up, dressing in black, leaving only at night, and murmuring about "dark forces," you may stir up interest and be able to open a "haunted" bed and breakfast, with *terrifyingly* reasonable rates.

Five Months Later

Swishing around town in a black cloak is not *not* fun, but it just seems to make everyone even more uncomfortable. Maybe you should carry a black cat around.

Six Months Later

Rumor has spread that the belligerent bridesmaid has possessed you and plans to open a gate to hell (or possibly Lane Bryant) in the house. Frightened, the townsfolk mobilize, and arrive at your door armed with shovels, pitchforks, and torches. They see the "Protected by Brinks Home Security" sticker on your front window and balk, not knowing that a threatening sticker is the extent of your home security. You decide you'd rather be safe than sorry and put the house on the market. Unloading real estate in *this* economy? Now *that's* scary.

Go to Therapy

It's always the same nightmare. You're at the bottom of a long staircase, wearing a flowing white nightgown. You're frightened, but you feel compelled to climb the staircase. As you ascend, you begin to hear voices whispering in a language you can't understand, and the shadows grow darker. Unseen shapes brush against you, even getting tangled in your hair, but you continue up the staircase, faster and faster until finally you arrive at a massive door. It's slightly ajar, but so huge it takes all your strength to push it open further. In the room is a man seated with his back to you. Ever more apprehensive, you approach—you *must* know who it is. You draw near and see that the man is your sixth-grade gym teacher. He's brandishing a pair of calipers, and cackles, "Skin fold test before the timed mile! And don't think you can take the algebra test in your underwear!" What does it *mean*? You make an appointment with a therapist to plumb the recesses of your psyche.

One Hour Later

Your therapist recommends that you try group therapy and makes an appointment for you, despite your objection that if you wanted to sit around listening to men being vulnerable, you'd stay home and listen to Fall Out Boy.

One Week Later

Ba-*zing*! You almost blew off group therapy but you're glad you didn't, because in your group is the most attractive man you have ever seen. He's just sitting there on a metal folding chair, an Adonis whose mother was an alcoholic. You don't even want to look directly *at* him, he's so handsome. The group moderator is careful to explain that dating within the group is *strongly discouraged*, but you don't plan to give up hope.

Two Weeks Later

It's your turn to speak, and you panic. Nightmares? That's not nearly crazy enough to stay in group therapy. They'll make you leave and you'll never see Hot Therapy Ben again. Without thinking, you start telling a completely fictional horror story about your upbringing—anything to keep you in group and near Hot Therapy Ben.

Four Weeks Later

"... and then when I was fourteen, my identical twin spontaneously combusted before my very eyes. . . ."

Seven Weeks Later

Hot Therapy Ben graduated, having finally accepted that it's not his fault his mother drank, it's his father's. Now that you're not in group together, you can date! He mentioned in passing the area of town he lives in, so you spend a lot of time there on the hunt.

Nine Weeks Later

Aha! You see Ben at a coffee shop and join him. You're flirting so hard your eyelids hurt, but he's not taking the bait. Finally, he tells you that you're a sweet, pretty girl, but that he just can't give you the care and attention someone with your traumatic background needs. He doesn't want to hurt you further. Somehow, it doesn't change his mind when you scream, "I made it all up! My parents weren't Satanists; they're barely Lutherans! I just thought you were hot!"

Watch a Horror Movie

You've been waiting for this for months. Stabbin' Sven Svensen, Norway's leading horror movie director and the inventor of the controversial "Nordic splatter" genre, has released his newest examination of the human spirit (and viscera). *Disemboweling Oslo*, the long-awaited sequel to *The Copenhagen Slasher* and *Everyone in Helsinki Is Dead*, has been reviewed as being "the scariest thing to come out of Scandinavia since Bjork's sense of self-importance." Your copy has finally arrived, in the limited-edition blood-red shrink wrap, and now that it's getting dark outside you're going to make some popcorn, rev up the DVD player, and get ready to absolutely wet yourself with terrified glee.

Twenty Minutes Later
This movie reminds you that, underneath all the socialized medicine and prosperity, Norwegians totally used to be Vikings.

Three Hours Later
That film was certainly vivid. You've gone to bed with all the lights on and a baseball bat next to you, but you're still unsettled.

One Week Later
Disemboweling Oslo struck a chord with you, or something. You've had night terrors every night since you watched it, and wake up screaming about twice per sleep cycle.

Two Weeks Later
You've tried everything to get the "kitchen scene" out of your head, but nothing works. You've tried getting drunk, you've tried breathing exercises, and you've

watched *Milo and Otis* so many times you can recite it, but the minute you fall asleep your mind goes right back to the moment when the killer approaches Ulrika with the pepper mill. . . . You've checked yourself in the mirror, and you look beyond haggard. If you're going to be up, you might as well make a few casseroles for the next few weeks' dinner and freeze them so the time isn't completely wasted.

Four Weeks Later

Detectives Rivera and Schultz arrive to have a word with you. It seems your pale, anxious appearance, coupled with the nightly screaming fits, have alarmed your neighbors. They decided to check your trash, and found the beef blood you drained off the eight pounds of ground beef you used to make Hamburger Helper meals for the next month. Alarmed, they called the police. You tell them that it's nothing, you just watched this really scary movie and it *got* to you, so you made a lot of food because you were up anyway. They seem skeptical, and take one of the casseroles to the lab for analysis.

Six Weeks Later

The lab report comes back, and as you told them, the casseroles contain only beef and no drifters who have recently gone missing. Rivera tells you you got lucky *this* time, but he knows what you're up to, and some day you'll slip up, and he'll come down on you like a ton of bricks. As he leaves, he pauses, and adds that you use way too much paprika.

Write a Novel

This summer, you're really going to do it. No more lying in the hammock with a legal pad and a dreamy expression just *thinking* about it; you're finally going to write the novel you've always dreamed of writing. This is it, the big one, the honest-yet-nuanced unfolding of the human condition that will make grown men weep. You've bought an old-timey clackety-clack typewriter and a tweed jacket with leather elbow patches, a ream of fancy onionskin paper, and a travel mug that reads "You Got the Write One Baby." Time to *create*.

Six Weeks Later

That was fast. Four hundred pages on man's desperation to preserve his faded memory of childhood innocence. Copied and sent to publishers.

Six Months Later

Cool! *What We Feared We Had Lost* is 967,273rd in sales on Amazon!

One Year Later

What We Feared We Had Lost is a runaway bestseller. Critics praise the restrained intensity of the language, and readers relate to the exquisitely drawn characters.

One Year, Six Months Later

You receive a huge advance for your upcoming second book, which the publishers expect to "glow with the luminous perception of Jonathan Franzen without the relentless condescension."

One Year, Eleven Months, Three Weeks Later

You haven't written a word, and the book is due next week. Panicked, you wash down a handful of No-Doz with a belt of whiskey, turn on the TV, and type. Everything that passes by goes in. Sparkling vampires, werewolves with feelings, teenage mothers releasing Top-40 hits, political revolt on Twitter, and through it all Barbara Walters asking everyone what went through their minds at the time. You title it *Decline and Fall for Dummies* and send it in.

Two Years, Three Months Later

The kindest review of your book refers to it as "what would happen if MTV had a miscarriage, then dressed it up for the Oscars." Shattered by the cruel press, you hide away in a hotel in Venice and drink yourself to death before the year is out.

Sixty Years Later

Society has reevaluated *Decline and Fall for Dummies,* and it is now hailed as a classic and is required reading for every high school student in America. Literary critics praise the elegant, straightforward satire as a witty indictment of the shallow, hysterical popular culture of the early twenty-first century, and credit its popularity for the now much lower crime rate and much higher standard of artistic expression. Because you never revised the will you made as a joke in college, the massive royalties go to the Green Party of Iowa, which now has a virtual lock on the state senate.

Try Out for Local Theater

Ever since your first stage appearance, as Helen Taft in your elementary school pageant *Our Nation's First Ladies*, you've been addicted to the limelight. You dabbled in acting in high school and college, but since then you've mostly satisfied your lust for fame with soulful renditions of "Let's Give 'Em Something to Talk About" on karaoke night. That said, you've never given up wanting to act again, and it looks like your chance might be coming up. Your local theatre company is putting on a production of *The Best Little Whorehouse in Texas*, and if your life has prepared you for one thing, it's to sing about being a kind-hearted prostitute with good business sense and broad regional appeal. You've done your vocal warmups and put on your movement clothes—time to show the director what you can do.

Fifteen Minutes Later

Your voice cracks on a high note of your go-to audition song, an ambitious one-voice rendition of the duet "The Boy Is Mine," as popularized by Brandy and Monica.

Four Hours Later

Are you kidding? Not cast at all? Not even "Featured Whore?"

Four Hours, Five Minutes Later

Oh, lah-dee-dah. Those who were not cast are welcome to be part of the production as the set crew. What a treat. You'll do it to show you're a professional, but you are not pleased.

One Week Later

You show up for crew duty and are assigned whorehouse detail work. Fine. You're going to show them; everything is going to be ever so slightly crooked, and the brocade on the wall will appear distinctly faded and worn.

Three Weeks Later

Your sabotage is going according to plan, when all of a sudden some yahoo carrying the lunchtime sandwich order slams the door on the way in. The ornamental longhorn skull you deliberately did a bad job nailing to the set wall comes loose and hits you in the face. You scream, and instinctively run backstage and hide. No one must see you. Later, as you try to patch yourself, you realize you didn't get your tuna salad on rye.

Twenty Years Later

The cow skull mangled your face, and you're not fit to be seen by human eyes. You've continued to live in the little theatre, hiding in prop rooms and sets, scavenging what food you can from the concession stand and leftover bagel trays. Local legend says you haunt the theatre—but who's haunting whom? They're not the ones who've had to see an aging Junior League revive *Oliver!* not once, but four times.

Join the Armed Forces

You'd like to be able to blame the recession for your recent employment dry spell, but it's really your fault. With your sticky fingers, lack of references, and resume consisting only of the phrase "GIT 'R DONE!" in 72-point font, you're not likely to make the cut at Souper Salad any time soon. You could probably crash at your aunt's indefinitely, but you've decided it's time to grow up and make something of yourself. You don't have the cash for night classes in phlebotomy, so you decide to do the American thing and join the armed services. You throw on an extra coat of Speed Stick to help you make that all-important good first impression, and drive over to the recruitment center.

One Hour Later

You flip through the brochures and settle on the Coast Guard. How hard can it be to guard a beach? You have visions of yourself tightening bikini ties, passing out sunscreen, and shooting sharks with high-powered artillery.

Three Months Later

Basic training was a more excruciatingly difficult physical workout than an '80s titty movie, but you made it to the end. You've been stationed aboard the USS *Ross Perot*, a small but independent-minded search-and-rescue boat.

Three Months, One Week Later

Due to your previously unknown debilitating seasickness, two things happen: you earn the nickname "Admiral Upchuck," and you receive a medical transfer to a lighthouse off the coast of northern Maine.

Four Months Later

You've eaten a clam, drunk a can of Narragansett, and seen a moose, so short of helping *Murder, She Wrote* heroine Jessica Fletcher unmask the killer you've done all Maine has to offer. Bored one night on duty, you start making shadow puppets in front of the beacon. Your crab, puppy dog, and finch appear enormous and majestic in the night sky.

Four Months, Four Hours Later

New Englanders are more skittish than they'd have you believe. Unbeknownst to you up in your phallic outpost, the townsfolk have seen your shadow puppets in the night sky and mistaken them for some form of supernatural activity. A folksy, crusty, New England–style panic breaks out, manifesting itself largely in the form of a run on chowder supplies and a number of calls to the Department of Homeland Security that begin with the phrase, "It's probably nothin', but the wife thinks sky critters are on the loose."

Five Months Later

The Coast Guard trades you to the Tennessee National Guard Reserve for a used floor buffer and a mostly full bottle of Pine-Sol. You are put to work racially profiling people in line for Graceland.

Do Some Soul Searching

Your job is going gangbusters. You're a top attorney at Boston's biggest corporate law firm, on track to make partner, and your skin's finally clearing up. You've even managed to find a special someone who can keep up with you in the bedroom as well as the boardroom. You thought you were perfectly content, but then you got an e-mail from a corporate headhunter offering you a position in Paris, City of Lights, fashion capital of the world, and home to some really exciting mergers and acquisitions. You're torn: comfort or adventure? The old or the new? The known or the unknown? Looks like you have a lot of soul-searching to do. . . .

One Week Later

You slowly walk along the beach. You've found a piece of driftwood, and every few steps you tap it thoughtfully against the sand. After a while, you pause to skip a few stones into the mighty Atlantic.

Two Weeks Later

You stare thoughtfully out the window at a rainstorm. The shadows of the droplets are reflected onto your pensive face, and from a distance it seems you are weeping.

Three Weeks Later

You make detailed lists of the pros and cons of each possible decision. In the end, they come out about even, and you sigh heavily, drop your pencil onto the table, and lay your head in your hands.

Four Weeks Later

You talk out your dilemma with an old and trusted friend. She tells you the truth as she sees it, not just what she thinks you want to hear. In the end, she tells you it looks like you'll just have to go with your heart.

Five Weeks Later

You sit on a park bench, facing a playground where children frolic and slowly drink a latte. You envy the children their innocence and freedom from responsibility.

Six Weeks Later

You pray on it.

Seven Weeks Later

You drink a glass of wine while staring into a roaring fire, occasionally shaking your head slightly at the complexity of it all.

Eight Weeks Later

You finally come to a decision, but unfortunately you spent so much time soul searching the offer from Paris is off the table. Additionally, you've been so dreamy and absent-minded the last two months your current job decides to let you go. Your relationship is in shambles, since you've spent weeks telling your boyfriend you were going through some transitions and he naturally assumed you were having an affair. Also the rent is late. How will you ever get your life back on track? Looks like you've got a lot of soul searching to do. . . .

Buy Some Land

There are certain things a man should just have. Some drinkin' whiskey, a huntin' dog, a shootin' gun, a smokin' hot wife, and some land to put it all on. Granted, you possess a weak liver, break out in hives around domestic animals, believe in gun control, and are as queer as a three-dollar bill, but it would be nice to have some land on which to enjoy your vitamins, allergy shots, no-kill mouse traps, and boyfriend. You drive outside of town and look at a plot for sale, and decide to buy it. You're feeling manlier already.

One Week Later

You go out to your land just to look at it and let it all wash over you, and get a big surprise. There are huge, elaborate crop circles all over the area. You don't know if it's the work of ghosts, aliens, or area teens, and you don't care. You're going to make some cash on it.

Two Weeks Later

It's amazing what kind of buzz you can get just from a few posts on old *X-Files* message boards. You set up a card table and cash box on the outskirts of the property, and charge $5 per slack-jawed yokel to stare at the mysterious crop circles. You're making a killing.

Six Weeks Later

Disaster. Just as you're approved for a small-business expansion loan to install railings and a handicapped-accessible ramp (damn ADA), you hear that the Mothman has been sighted in a neighboring county. Attendance drops sharply at your crop circles, since you can see crop circles any old time but the Mothman is famously skittish and might decamp at any moment. You're losing money fast and need a plan.

Eight Weeks Later

You decide to one-up this Mothman and recapture your audience by staging an appearance by the Jersey Devil, played, for union reasons, by yourself. You stop by the costume shop, and the only "devilish" costume they have is a sorority-style "sexy" devil, complete with mini-cape and high-heeled hooves. Beggars can't be choosers, and you're a relatively small-boned man, so you decide to make it work. You don the costume and slip out at night, planning to leap and cavort near the farms that edge your property and produce some "sightings." No one seems to be out and about, so you move closer to one of the houses and start howling while you hop about. An easily startled farm wife sees a devil-like creature hopping around in her yard and does what any sensible farm wife would do: drops you with three well-placed shots from a .38. The next day, when your body is recovered and identified, your family has to pay a small fortune to suppress the news that you were shot to death in drag on someone's beet farm.

Change Religions

You've been drifting and aimless since the band broke up. You really thought "Nigerian Scam" was your ticket out of this one-horse burg, but your dreamy ska hooks and piercing vocals failed to find an audience, and the members decided to cut their losses and go their separate ways. You've got a lot of questions, and *The United Methodist Hymnal* just isn't giving you the answers you need this time. You decide to explore other religions, and start by stopping by the Church of Scientology card table outside the fabric store. If it doesn't work out, you can always pick up some rickrack to breathe some new life into that old tablecloth.

One Hour Later

The Scientology representative doing your e-meter reading and giving you the *Reader's Digest* Condensed Books version of *Dianetics* seems to be making a lot of sense. You always thought Scientology was a glorified Dungeons and Dragons plotline followed by misfits and lunatics, but you never really considered how *fun* that sounded.

Three Years Later

Everything's coming up thetans! You've made a lot of progress since joining the Church of Scientology, and even found a husband. Because he's relatively high up in the organization, you were able to be married at the Hollywood Scientology Center—and as a special surprise, the ceremony was officiated by Kirstie Alley, who looks wonderful for her age. (She's over sixty!) You're expecting your first child, and look forward to raising a cradle Scientologist.

Three Years, One Week Later

Hold the phone. Apparently you're supposed to give birth without drugs, but also without making a sound, so that "negative energy" doesn't get into the baby? You'll see what you can do, but you're not optimistic.

Three Years, Six Months Later

You gave it the old college try. You spent the first seven hours of labor gritting your teeth and imagining a field full of flowers. During the next few hours, you moved on to graphic hand gestures and breathing loudly. You've done reasonably well, but as the baby's head pushes through you can bear it no longer, so you fill your lungs, throw back your head, and bellow: *"Motherfuckingshitballpissasssonofabitch!"* Nothing ever felt so good.

Four Years Later

People have failed to give silent birth before, but never quite so colorfully. You and your allegedly negative-energy-filled baby are expelled from the Church of Scientology. Back at a spiritual square one, you decide to give the Jews for Jesus a whirl. You're not Jewish and uncertain about Jesus, but you hear they'll take just about everyone.

Hold a Séance

Fun has been revised downward since the recession began. In the heady days of 2007, a Friday night meant champagne bubble baths at Madame Dao's Pleasure Junction before watching opera from the all-you-can-eat-lobster box at the Met. Now it means splitting a bottle of Arbor Mist with your landlady while watching the USA "Up All Night" movie, *Canadian Bacon*. As you portion out the last few ounces of peachy goodness, you and Mrs. Fernandez decide to really dial the night up to eleven and hold a séance to finally ask John Candy those burning questions: "Was Michael Moore always insufferable? Was there any truth to the rumors about a Quebecois independence–themed sequel, *Poutine*? And ultimately, was it all worth it?" You hastily drew a pentagram on the floor with a magic marker while Mrs. Fernandez lit a red candle, and you were ready to begin.

One Minute Later

Thanks to your adorable little Georgia drawl, instead of John Candy the beloved actor you summon the demon J'ahnkan-Di, Knight of Wrath and Breaker of the Eight Seals.

Two Minutes Later

J'ahnkan-Di assures you that Michael Moore was always insufferable and that *Poutine* never got past some rough storyboarding. He then possesses Mrs. Fernandez and goes forth to spread corruption and despair o'er the land.

Five Minutes Later

Paris is burning.

Ten Minutes Later

Volcanoes open in the earth and pour out fire, killing millions. Blood pours from every mirror in the Vatican. Earthquakes destroy Jerusalem. Thunderous waves tear at the coasts. Giant scorpions pour forth from the sea and devour grown men whole. A dark fire covers the sky from horizon to horizon. Animals claw at their own flesh. Infants vomit swarms of hornets and stinging flies. The faithful pray in vain. Clouds gather and let serpents fall in lieu of rain. All the devils of Hell rise up and make terrible war on the living.

Fifteen Minutes Later

All is fire, all is agony, all is death. The Moral of the Story: Go to college out of state so your vowels get ironed out and you don't end the world by talking like a hillbilly.

Put a Bumper Sticker on Your Car

Your grandmother's passing has been tough, but when God closes a door, he opens a window. Specifically, one of four power windows attached to the '98 Jetta that she left you in her will. Sure you've always been more of a Volvo guy, but it's still a pretty sweet car. Low mileage, tinted windows, spacious legroom—what more could you ask for? Well, your grandmother to be alive again, for one, but car-wise—nothing! The car would be perfect if it weren't for a small, yet unsightly scratch on the back right bumper, which you've decided to cover with a bumper sticker. Like pancake batter on an acne scar, it's not the best cover-up, but it'll work. Armed with a five-dollar bill and a dope sense of humor, you drive to the mall and start perusing the bumper sticker carousel at Spencer's Gifts. You take a step back from the freshly applied bumper sticker and pause for a moment to enjoy your handiwork—a good old "Honk If You're Horny" sticker. You wish your grandma were here to see this.

Fifty-Six Minutes Later
While driving home from the mall, you get your first honk and wonder if life will ever be any more wonderful than this exact moment.

Fifty-Six Minutes and Ten Seconds Later
You get your second honk.

Fifty-Six Minutes and Twenty Seconds Later
Third honk.

Fifty-Six Minutes and Thirty Seconds Later
Fourth honk.

Fifty-Six Minutes and Forty Seconds Later
Fifth honk.

Fifty-Eight Minutes Later
This is . . . regrettable.

One Month Later
As you're driving down the highway, the car next to you starts wildly honking. Numb from the 70,000 horny automobilists you've heard for the past month, you let out a heavy sigh and give a half-hearted wave without even looking over.

One Month and Five Seconds Later
Interpreting your wave as the go-ahead to merge into your lane, the inexperienced sixteen-year-old driver in the car next to yours jerks her wheel to the right, hits your car, and sends you both flying into the Jersey wall.

One Month and Four Minutes Later
Having regained consciousness, you get out of the car, stumble, and fall into the arms of a State Trooper. "Sir, can you hear me?" the State Trooper asks, "Are you hurt? The young lady said you motioned for her to move into your lane, what happened?"

One Month, Four Minutes, and Fourteen Seconds Later
"I thought she was horny," you grunt through the throbbing pain in your head. As a look of disturbed confusion washes over the trooper's face, you, both irritated by the situation and now starting to lose consciousness again, shout, "I . . . THOUGHT . . . SHE WAS . . . *HORNY*," before crumbling at the Trooper's feet.

Six Months Later
You're sentenced to eight months in jail for lewd acts with a minor.

Buy Urban Chickens

Urban chickens are on the forefront of the über-green, militant eco-hipster movement. You buy your eggs from a grocery store? WAY TO SUPPORT BIG OVA FARMING AND DOOM THOUSANDS OF FOWL TO LIVE IN TINY LITTLE CHICKEN AUSCHWITZES, YOU FASCIST! You can buy a Groupon for a walking tour and a massage, listen to The Decemberists, and take all the yoga classes Portland has to offer, but you'll never be a *real* twenty/thirty-something elitist urbanite until the frittatas you serve at brunch are made with eggs straight from the hutch on the fire escape. Still sore about missing that whole "geek chic" thing that was hot for a second there in the late '00s, you vowed not to miss out on the urban chicken trend. The second it hit the blogs, you made a beeline to Chinatown, bought four live chickens, and haven't looked back since.

One Hour Later

Now back in your apartment, you herd your newly acquired chickens onto the fire escape, put out a bowl of water, toss out a handful of Triscuits, and congratulate yourself for being so "new urban."

One Week Later

You have now named all four of your chickens: Darfur, Rwanda, Gaza, and Congo (so you always remember).

One Month Later

Congo lays a stillborn egg and you, Darfur, Rwanda, and Gaza are really there for her. The entire experience is bonding.

Two Months Later

You start letting your chickens sleep at the foot of your bed when there's inclement weather or a good guest on *Jimmy Kimmel Live!*

Three Months Later

The meal ticket/pet line is blurred even further when you begin dressing your chickens up in Bedazzled jackets and running errands with them tucked into an oversized Louis Vuitton handbag.

Three Months and One Week Later

A picture of you offering Congo a forkful of your eggs Benedict while Gaza nurses a mimosa at Sunday Fun Day brunch circulates on the Internet, catching the eye of PETA (and the Health Department).

Three Months, One Week, and One Day Later

PETA launches a full-fledged attack against you, vilifying you online and sending a few Wellesley girls swathed in armpit hair and outrage to picket outside of your apartment. You try to disperse the protesters by launching a volley of Congo's fresh eggs at them and the resulting fracas eventually leads to the Health Department taking your chickens away.

Three Months, One Week, and Two Days Later

We have two words: Urban Bears. Your heart will go on.

Run for Political Office

You were hesitant to leave the fast-paced, dog-eat-dog life you led in Chicago behind for small-town living, but the move has turned out to be an absolute blessing. Here in Thermopolis, "the hottest little city in Wyoming," you met your loving wife and turned the struggling local daily into a respected local news source. (All it took was replacing *Doonesbury* with the daily Jumble.) You feel it's time you gave back to this place that has given you so very much, and so you've announced your intention to run for mayor. You're sure your compassionate conservatism will keep Thermopolis growing and thriving, and you're ready to take your case to the voters.

One Day Later

The liberal who owns the video rental store asks you what's so "compassionate" about your conservatism: "Are you gonna, like, fire a warning shot at our rights first?" You poke him in the eye and shoot up to an 87 percent approval rating.

One Week Later

The campaign is running smoothly, despite an awkward exchange with a reporter—apparently the radical right-wing John Birch Society isn't a conservationist group.

Two Weeks Later

All hell has broken loose. Some damn snoop has found out why you left Chicago and leaked it to the media. You had hoped you had left your past "film" career behind, but alas. The connection has been made, and now everyone knows you made a number of "erotic dramas" under the name Rod Hardman. You protest that they aren't *pornography*, they're *erotic dramas*, and have very complex and developed plots—it just happens that these plots generally involve full frontal nudity and suicide blondes named Sharlayne.

One Month Later

It's no use. You lose the election in a landslide, which the local gossip rag reports as "Loses Erection by a Landslide."

Five Years Later

You were hesitant to leave the sleepy, gentle life you knew in small-town Wyoming for the hustle and bustle of Los Angeles, but the move has turned out to be an absolute blessing. After your campaign collapsed, you were contacted by a representative from Red, White, and ESPECIALLY Blue Productions, an adult video company specializing in erotic political parodies. Since your electoral defeat, you've starred in a number of naughty satires, including *Hail to My Beef*, *Supreme Courtship*, *The Executive's Branch*, *The Ducockis Campaign*, and most memorably, *House Minority Beaver*.

Shoplift

It's your worst nightmare, but then again, you were never that imaginative. You've run to the deli around the corner from your apartment to grab the essentials (Pert Plus, Necco Wafers, and double-sided tape) and while in line, you realize that you forgot your wallet and only have five bucks on you. You can cover any two of the items, but your hair looks like shit, you haven't had dinner, and you'd really like to get this collage done. You have to put something back, unless you just slip the Necco Wafers into your waistband and act really happy to see Mr. Kim. Unfortunately, Mr. Kim is not fooled and after giving you a long lecture about how the NYPD and your ancestors would be very disappointed, he snaps your picture and adds you to the wall of people no longer allowed in the store. It was embarrassing, sure, but at least you didn't blink and ruin the photo.

One Day Later

Trying to make peace, you send Mr. Kim a $30 gift card to The Macaroni Grill with your apologies.

Two Days Later

You check your mail and discover that Mr. Kim has sent the gift card back to you cut up with a note that says he can't be bought.

One Week Later

Your lifetime ban goes from inconvenient to genuinely serious one night when you desperately need to zip out for Q-Tips and ant traps and can't just pop into Mr. Kim's. Instead, you have to hoof it ten blocks uptown to the nearest Whole Foods and get cruelty-free combs and a little device that gently ushers ants out of your apartment and gives them the address of a nearby safe house. Damn those Necco Wafers. (Addendum: need Q-Tips, ant traps, *and* Necco Wafers.)

Two Weeks Later

After a three-day-old chimichanga starts stirrin' up trouble south of the border, you discover, to your horror, that you're out of Imodium. Walking ten blocks in this state is not an option. Making it *downstairs* is going to be touch-and-go. Frantic, you approach a brightly, but scantily clad woman on the street and ask if she'll do you a favor for ten bucks: if she could run into Mr. Kim's and pick you up some Imodium, she can pick herself up something of equal or lesser value and keep the change. As you hand her the money, two plain-clothes police officers swoop in and arrest you for solicitation. It does not help your case when you lose bowel control in the police cruiser.

Two Months Later

At your trial, you plead no contest and agree to start going to Sex Addicts Anonymous meetings.

Three Months Later

Although your friends and family think that you're a sexual deviant and you still have to walk ten blocks for Necco Wafers, this cloud does have a silver lining: a lifetime of Saturdays spent in a church basement surrounded by raging nymphomaniacs.

Buy a Motorcycle

It's three o'clock in the morning and you're wide awake because your next-door neighbor's experimental noise band is laying down tracks for their new album "Grindcore Cabaret." You try going over to ask them to keep it down, but they're too stoned to understand what you're saying and give you a bag of Andy Capp's Hot Fries out of confusion. While you appreciate the gesture, you're also slowly going out of your mind from insomnia, so you decided to buy a motorcycle to rev in the alley and fight fire with fire.

One Day Later

After the fifth take of the track "Kyle's Screams," you get out of bed and start revving your engine. Instead of breaking up the recording session, your neighbor comes out and asks if you could keep it up because it's giving the track a really gritty sound.

Two Days Later

As long as you have it, you might as well ride it.

One Month Later

You've gotten really into riding your hog. You don't know which you like better: the cool breeze of the open road or all the lip licking soccer moms do as you whiz by. You get really obsessed with motorcycle culture, track down your local chapter of the Hell's Angels, and ask what it takes to be a part of the crew. A man named "Meat Stick" tells you that it ain't easy, you're going to endure a "pretty brutal" initiation period and may not survive. You show your enthusiasm by shattering a beer bottle over your head.

One Month and One Week Later

You arrive at the Hell's Angels' watering hole, Dante's Inferno and Sports Bar, ready to prove your manhood. The bikers circle you, arms folded and expressions grim, and announce that it's time for the first trial. One man reaches into his bag and pulls out a sealed plastic bag with a live goldfish inside. He thrusts it toward you and simply says, "Swallow it." You feel like this is starting slow, but you do it anyway.

One Month and Two Weeks Later

Trial number two: You're ordered to steal a rival motorcycle gang's mascot. You're pretty amped, figuring it's going to be a wolf or a cobra, but are disappointed, and somewhat confused, when it turns out to be a house cat.

One Month and Three Weeks Later

Trial number three: You're told you'll be doing a little vandalism. You ask if you should bring your own bat for the window smashing and are told, "No, but a couple extra rolls of Charmin never go to waste!"

One Month and Four Weeks Later

The final trial that will prove your fearlessness: streak down the block—*AND ALL THE WAY BACK!!!* After you do this, the bikers reveal that they're not really bikers at all, but disguised Yalies whose fraternity hazing is to haze someone else. Looks like they're all getting into Sigma Chi, so they buy you a beer.

Start a Blog

You thought managing an Anthropologie and running your own letterpress Etsy store would be fulfilling, but you need another outlet for your creativity. You just have *so* many ideas about design and you really want to share them with the world. For example, did you know that you can turn vintage autoharp strings into kicky bracelets just by wrapping them around your wrist and securing them with baker's twine? Or that in only thirty-seven easy steps, you can transform a discarded condom box into a keen pinhole camera? Has everyone *seen* how good your high bun looks today? You decide the best way to get out your message of almost-affordable chic is to start a lifestyle blog. Not like a *blog* blog, but, you know, like a sophisticated Internet place for ideas and fun. Definitely feminist, but not like *feminist* feminist. For pretty feminists! You decide to call it BigWorldLittleGirl.com, throw on some cute reading glasses, and start blogging away.

Ten Minutes Later

You upload an Instagram photo of yourself walking your pug, Windsor, in your new Frye boots while eating a gluten-free cupcake. You know, so people can see what you're all about. You get 113 comments from people around the world telling you how gosh darn cute you look. Awww! Thanks, guys!

One Month Later

After a photo of you and your boyfriend (a.k.a. The Boy) riding a tandem bicycle with Windsor, your pug, in the front basket goes viral, Urban Outfitters contacts you about buying ad space on your blog for their new line of fixed-gear bicycles designed by Mark Ronson. And they're just the first. Other sponsorship offers come rolling in from

Nikon, TOMS shoes, Luna Bar, and West Elm. With the money rolling in, you quit your job at Anthropologie and devote yourself to blogging full time.

Six Months Later

After ironing your collection of whimsical skirts one night, you accidentally leave the iron on and burn your brownstone down. Windsor and The Boy are fine, thank God, but while they rebuild your house, you have to move back in with your parents in—*gulp*—the suburbs.

One Year Later

You're heartbroken when The Boy's job transfers him to their Singapore office. You briefly consider going with him, but Portland is who you *are*.

One Year and Three Months Later

Windsor gets tapeworms from the photo shoot you two did at the pumpkin patch.

One Year and Four Months Later

The blog comments start dwindling the more photos you post of yourself in an oversized Adidas T-shirt, crying, and cleaning up Windsor's mess. Your sponsors pull out when you upload a video of yourself singing along to Jewel's "Pieces of Me" and eating a sponge cake with your hands. Your empire is crumbling, and you don't know what to do next. Lord knows you burned a few bridges at Anthropologie....

One Year and Six Months Later

Paxil starts sponsoring you and you reinvent the blog as a suicide prevention community. You knew you'd come out on top.

 **Have Team Spirit**

Who says school spirit is just for high schoolers and college kids? From where you're standing, a thirty-seven-year-old man getting his master's degree in social work has just as much of a right to root for the Alabama Crimson Tide as anyone else! In fact, you and some of the other guys in the social work program decided to really show your school spirit for the game against Auburn and paint your bare chests to spell out "roll tide." For the record, you are the "O." You're painted, you're tailgated, and you're ready for the game to start. ROLL TIDE!!!

One Hour Later
It sure is nippy out here. You put on another layer of grease paint and double down on the Miller Lite for warmth.

Three Days Later
The "sniffles" you developed on the way home from the game (ROLL TIDE!!!) have developed into a full-blown flu. You have a fever, your throat hurts, your body aches, and you can't stop shivering long enough to fall asleep, so you down some NyQuil. The cooling action relieves your symptoms, while the powerful sedative knocks you the fuck out. You're grateful for the first full night's sleep you've had in days.

Four Days Later
You're feeling better, but not *well*. You take some NyQuil before bed again, figuring one more good night's sleep should do it.

Five Days Later

You've fully recovered from the flu, but that doesn't mean you're going to stop knocking back that sweet, sweet Quil. You love the way it sends you into a deep twilight state of being and you're beginning to acquire a taste for it as well. You've taken to mixing it with 7-Up and grenadine and calling it an "antihistini."

Six Days Later

You spend the whole day robo-tripping your balls off, rolling back and forth on the kitchen floor, enjoying the texture of the hooked rug.

Two Weeks Later

Recognizing you have a problem and are addicted to cough syrup, you try to join Alcoholics Anonymous, but when you stand up and say, "Hi, my name is Clarence and I'm not really an alcoholic, but I'm drinking three bottles of cough syrup a day," they laugh you off the dais. Well, you gave recovery a good college try—time to stir a bottle of Robitussin into a bottle of whipping cream, call the result a "Purple People Eater" and drink it directly from the bowl. You can manage your demons yourself.

Seven Years Later

Turns out you couldn't handle your own demons and you spend most days swinging a bent nine iron at pterodactyls only you can see behind the CEFCO mini-mart. ROLL TIDE!!!

Throw the Old Pigskin

On a lazy Sunday afternoon when the weather is crisp, the sun is warm, and the game isn't on for a few more hours, nothing beats cracking open a few beers, heading out back and throwin' the old pigskin around for a while. There's no pressure from the wife, coach isn't riding you to score a touchdown and play 110 percent—it's just you and a buddy rappin' about trucks, chicks, and whether or not the Bengals are going to go all the way this year. Women have bubble baths, children have Saturday cartoons, and you have this moment: standing in the back yard in your best windbreaker, Bud Light in your left hand, and pigskin in your right. It's like heaven without the dress code.

Ten Minutes Later

Your son comes out and asks if he can join. You're just getting ready to tell your buddy about the new Girls of Texaco calendar at work, so you tell him no and to run on into the house and ask if his mother needs any help setting the table.

Twenty Minutes Later

You hear a sound and wonder if your son is using the yard instead of the toilet again and turn to look just as your buddy throws the ball. It smacks you square in the groin and you fall backward into a mud puddle clutching your battered nards.

Two Days Later

Unbeknownst to you, your son was annoyed at not being allowed to play catch and filmed your middle-aged antics in revenge. He posts the excerpt in which you get hit in the groin and fall in the mud to

YouTube under the title "Football Retard Follies." It goes viral almost immediately.

Two Weeks Later

Tom Brady, star quarterback for the New England Patriots, sees the video and feels sorry for you. He contacts your son through his YouTube account and asks if he can meet the "brave little soldier" who loves football so much, despite his special needs. Your son happily offers to arrange a meet-and-greet with you and Brady the next time the quarterback is in the area.

One Month Later

The Patriots are in town to play the Bengals. You get a knock on the door and are flabbergasted to see Tom Brady and Gisele Bundchen. "Hey, tiger!' Brady says, "Mind if we come in?" Speechless, you step back so they can enter and stumble on the edge of the carpet. Brady and Bundchen exchange a knowing smile. "Easy there, killer," Brady says as he steadies you. "We might need you against the Saints next week!" An awkward exchange ensues, culminating in Brady offering to have a picture made with you sitting on his lap.

One Month and One Week Later

A friend finally forwards you a link to the YouTube video and all the pieces start to fall into place. You send your son to military school and the photo of you on Tom Brady's lap as your Christmas card.

Make Your Own Movie

You finally have a reason to start that Warhol-esque art film you've been meaning to make: the Montgomery County Civic Pride Jamboree! This year, the city council has challenged the public to create short films about what makes Montgomery County special. The winner gets a $100 gift certificate good at any participating locally owned business and a key to the city. The prize is as good as yours. Instead of doing the usual pedestrian montage of puppies, babies, returning soldiers, and an economically revitalized downtown area, you're going to challenge people's preconceptions with an outside-the-box tour de force of cinematic greatness. Get the popcorn!

One Day Later

You recruit a few actors from the junior college's theater department, rent a camera from the library, and start filming. You have to shoot the final scene seventeen times and one of the actors gets heatstroke, but you know how to push a performer to get a good scene.

Three Weeks Later

It's the night of the Civic Pride Jamboree and your epic, *Untitled with Woman and Violence (Montgomery County Pride)*, gets the coveted final slot in the schedule. You're still not happy with the claymation scene, but everything else is pretty topnotch.

Three Weeks and Two Hours Later

It premieres and the citizens of Montgomery County are subjected to forty-five minutes of quick cuts among a sobbing nude woman curled up on the linoleum floor, a child jumping rope while chanting the Latin mass, and an elderly dog awkwardly scratching dead grass over its waste. When the movie ends, you expect applause but are greeted instead with an uncomfortable silence, eventually broken by the emcee saying, "Well . . . help yourself to cake!"

Three Weeks and Two Days Later

You are surprised when a sheriff's deputy shows up at your door and arrests you on obscenity charges. It turns out Montgomery County wasn't ready for your art and a group of concerned mothers called the sheriff's department and demanded your head. "*Someone* has to be held accountable!"

Six Weeks Later

On the day of your trial, you arrive in the courtroom nude except for panties marked "Wednesday" and an American flag worn as a cape. You deliver a ringing oration on the beauty and sacredness of free speech. The judge agrees with you, but finds you in contempt of court for showing up to his courtroom looking like Captain America's confused younger brother.

Eight Weeks Later

You get 120 hours of community service for your contempt charge. You can't say you enjoy clearing dead animals off highway on-ramps, but you're getting some *great* footage for your next film!

Start a Podcast

One of the best things about being a Reagan Baby is having grown up with the 1990s cult classic TV show *Mystery Science Theater 3000*. *Mystery Science Theater 3000* (or "MST3K") was a comedy/sci-fi show in which a man and his robot sidekicks added sarcastic commentary to low-budget, low-quality science fiction movies. It's the best thing Western civilization has done since Christianity. One day you had an idea: Why not produce a podcast where you comment on an episode of MST3K, as they comment on the movie, and call it *Mystery Science Theater 6000*? You genuinely can't tell if this idea is only funny to you, but it's worth a shot.

One Month Later

It turns out it's not just funny to you, and your podcast becomes a cult darling, much like the original show.

Six Months Later

The podcast does so well that you're invited to attend the semiannual Comicon convention in Racine, Wisconsin.

Eight Months Later

You arrive at your table at Comicon and realize you've got a prime spot—a table next to Kevin Sorbo, TV's Hercules, and directly across from Quentin Tarantino, who is here to promote his new project, a blaxploitation remake of *Breakfast at Tiffany's* with ninjas.

Eight Months and Two Hours Later

You bond with your neighbor Kevin Sorbo and start throwing promotional pens at Tarantino. Every time Quentin yells, "QUIT IT!" you and Sorbo duck and giggle under the table.

Eight Months and Four Hours Later

You and Kevin Sorbo sneak into the bathroom and call Quentin Tarantino pretending to be Pam Grier. You make it all the way to agreeing to be in his next picture before you can't take it anymore and you and Sorbo burst into laughter. You go back to your tables to find Quentin standing there with his arms crossed. "NOT COOL, YOU *GUYS*."

Eight Months and Eight Hours Later

After a long day at the Con, your new best friend, Kevin Sorbo, suggests you hit a few bars. You readily agree and before long you're going shot-for-shot with TV's Hercules.

Eight Months and Nineteen Hours Later

You wake up in an alley fuzzy headed with the taste of vomit in your mouth. You manage to stand up and take out your wallet to see if you have enough cab fare to get back to the hotel. You open your wallet to find that your cash and credit cards are gone. All that remains is a folded-up five-by-seven glossy of Kevin Sorbo with the following note on the back: "Hey Bro. I really did have a good time hanging out with you yesterday, but my residuals are practically nothing. I'm sure you understand. Good luck with the podcast.—Kevin" As you stand in the alley considering your next move, a cackling Quentin Tarantino pulls up on a Segway, shouts, "Sayonara, bitches!" and rides off into the sunset. All in all, a pretty good convention.

Take Ballroom Dance Lessons

As good as your wedding was overall, there was one enormously embarrassing moment: your first dance. You can see it like it was yesterday. The crowd in the Marriott ballroom parted, the disco ball descended, and Boyz II Men's "I Swear" started pumping through the speakers. It's the moment every little girl dreams of. Unfortunately, you have the rhythm and grace of a moose with arthritic hips and spent the entire dance jerking uneasily in a small circle and stepping on your husband's feet. You never really appreciated how long "I Swear" was until that moment. That's why it was so sweet when for your first anniversary, your husband signed you both up for ballroom dance lessons. Time to cut a rug!

One Week Later

Your dance instructor, Bev, is exactly what you'd expect a dance instructor named Bev to look like: ridden hard and put away wet. You can tell she was probably beautiful when she was younger, but years of stiff competition and doors slamming in her face have left her a withered shell of what she once was. Hell of a dancer though.

One Month Later

After a couple of sessions, you don't seem to be getting any better. Bev takes a special interest in you and asks you to stay after class. She looks you up and down, takes a long drag of her Pall Mall and says, "Kid, it ain't gonna be fun, it ain't gonna be pretty, but by the time I'm done with you, you'll either be a dancer or a pile of dead bones. What d'ya say?" Hypnotized by the rhythmic batting of her false lashes, you agree.

Six Months Later

After months of long nights in the studio struggling to keep up as Bev barks "FIVE! SIX! SEVEN! EIGHT!" and bangs the end of a Swiffer on the floor, you have blossomed into the best goddamn dancer southern Ohio has ever seen. Bev is so proud she arranges for you and your husband to audition for a talent scout from Carnival Cruise Lines. You nail the audition and are offered a job, which you happily accept. Bev gives you a bony, smoky hug and tells you to "live the dream."

Eight Months Later

Everything is bocce board and free lobster buffets until your ship is rammed and boarded by pirates. You assume it's just another shipboard activity until they shoot the porter in the head.

Nine Months Later

After plundering the ship, the pirates abduct you and your husband. You're unclear why, until the pirate captain explains that they thought it would be a "real gas" to put on a shipboard production of *The Pirates of Penzance*. "You know, pirates and all." You're skeptical at first, but the first production is so much fun you decide to stick around and work your way through the whole Gilbert and Sullivan catalog. You wish Bev could be here to see this.

Enter a Radio Contest

You're driving along I-35 in your Toyota Camry when the DJs on Z-104 (DJ Mike and Skid Mark) announce that they're giving away the chance of a lifetime: the opportunity to spend a week as Sheryl Crow's roadie and interview her for their morning show, *Breakfast of Champions*. You get so excited at the thought of meeting your idol Sheryl Crow that you briefly lose control of the car and drive it into a ditch. Wasting no time, you leap from the wreckage and run to the highway emergency phone. You've got a call to make.

Thirty Seconds Later
"Hello, Z-104?! I can name that Sheryl Crow B-side in six notes!"

Thirty-Eight Seconds Later
"'Hard to Make a Stand'!" You get the trivia question right and win the Sheryl Crow showcase showdown. Within a few days, the radio station sends you your tour itinerary, a bus ticket to Santa Barbara, and a few DJ Mike and Skid Mark's *Breakfast of Champions* T-shirts in XXL.

Three Weeks Later
You meet up with the tour in Santa Barbara and are eager to show your devotion to Sheryl by being the best roadie you can be. It actually turns out that roadies have a pretty aggressive union, so your roadie tasks are boiled down to running down to the corner for smokes and awkwardly standing around the craft service table. You don't actually get to hang out with Sheryl Crow, but you know she's near and that's enough for you.

Three Weeks and Five Days Later

After spending most of the week flipping through old *Rolling Stones* and being bored senseless, you find out that you'll be interviewing Sheryl the following day at the last stop on her tour: a bold and not entirely thought-out appearance at the Burning Man festival. You'll only have fifteen minutes to make a good first impression. The stakes have never been higher.

Four Weeks Later

At Burning Man, you spend the whole day nervously pacing in the hot sun, rehearsing your questions for Sheryl. The extreme heat mixed with the fact that you haven't had anything to eat or drink all day for fear that you'd throw it back up leaves you dangerously dehydrated by nightfall. By the time the festival's giant wicker man is set ablaze, you're so delirious from dehydration that you think the burning man is some kind of Guy Fawkes effigy and run through the tent city screaming, "TREASON! DEFEND THE KING!" You don't get to conduct your interview with Sheryl because you're too busy warning Parliament that there is mutiny afoot. You mail the mini-recorder you had been given to interview Sheryl back to Z-104 with a note of apology. Unbeknownst to you, you accidentally turned it on during your freak-out and recorded a good portion of it.

Two Months Later

You yelling "FOR GOD AND ENGLAND!" has become DJ Mike and Skid Mark's favorite sound bite and they pepper it in their morning show *liberally*.

Conclusion

As we have seen, human lives are essentially short morality plays cranked out by the dozen by a writer's room staffed by O. Henry, H. P. Lovecraft, and Benny Hill. Maybe this comforts you because you believe in "fate," or maybe you find it disturbing because you'd like to think your successes are your own, and not the result of a woman in Christchurch finally cutting down the lime tree in her yard that she just *hates*. You can try to draw a moral from all this if you want, something in the don't sweat the small stuff / don't worry, be happy / everything I really need to know I learned in court-ordered anger management genre, but there's not much of a point. You can have inner peace coming out your ears, but the gods are still rolling the dice up there, and there's precious little you can do. If, however, you insist that your entertainment teach you something, consider this point. If what seems like a good idea so often goes wrong, then what seems like a bad idea must at least occasionally go wondrously, gloriously *well*. So if the mood strikes you, cash out your 401(k), hitchhike to Atlantic City, and go on a bender to end all benders, pausing only to take in a matinee performance of Paula Poundstone's one-woman production of *Steel Magnolias*. You'll probably wind up broke and alone with only a throbbing liver and a novelty oversized geometric vest for your trouble, but there's a nonzero chance you'll meet a princess—or a hooker named Pryncess—and live happily ever after.

Until the asteroid hits you.

ABOUT THE AUTHORS

Meghan Rowland and Chris Turner-Neal are the authors of *The Misanthrope's Guide to Life* and *Brainwashing for Beginners*. They avoid having to face the consequences of their actions by behaving erratically and changing their travel plans without warning. Together, they write the award-winning comedy blog, *www.2birds1blog.com*, which has been recognized by NPR, the *Washington Post*, and the Blogger's Choice Awards. Meghan lives in Washington, DC, and Chris lives in Philadelphia, PA.

DAILY BENDER

Want Some More?

Hit up our humor blog, The Daily Bender, to get your fill of all things funny—be it subversive, odd, offbeat, or just plain mean. The Bender editors are there to get you through the day and on your way to happy hour. Whether we're linking to the latest video that made us laugh or calling out (or bullshit on) whatever's happening, we've got what you need for a good laugh.

If you like our book, you'll love our blog. (And if you hated it, "man up" and tell us why.) Visit The Daily Bender for a shot of humor that'll serve you until the bartender can.

Sign up for our newsletter at
www.adamsmedia.com/blog/humor
and download our Top Ten Maxims No Man Should Live Without.